# Teach
# the Bahá'í Faith
# With Ease

## V. Mitra Gopaul

UnityWorks.com
Newmarket, ON

Published by UnityWorks.com
          Upper Canada Postal Outlet
          Box 21541
          Newmarket, Ontario Canada L3Y 8J1

Printed in Canada



**Canadian Cataloguing in Publication Data**

Gopaul, V. Mitra
    Teach the Bahá'í Faith With Ease


Includes bibliographical references and index.
ISBN: 0-9682976-0-9


    1. Bahá'í Faith. I. Title.

BP365.G66 1997          297.9'375          C97-901219-8




Copy editor: Pat Verge
Cover designer: Ike Bennett
Illustrator: Evan Long

*Dedicated to all teachers of the Bahá'í Faith*

## By the same author

Personal Computers in the Bahá'í Faith
C Programming in the MVS Environment
IBM Mainframe Programmer's Desk Reference
Developing C/C++ Software in the OS/2 Environment
OS/2 Programmer's Desk Reference
DB2 2.1 for OS/2 Made Easy

# Contents

# Foreword

Warmest greetings Earthlings! I am Yágnü (pronounced yaaganew, which means "heavenly bird" in my native planet of Titron) from the Bahá'í Era Project, Concourse on High. I remember very well how excited I was at the first interview when I was shown the plans for the Lesser Peace, Entry by Troops, Mass Conversion, the Bahá'í World Commonwealth, The Most Great Peace, and the Golden Age. Up here, every one talks about the Bahá'í Era with the greatest excitement. It is so cool! (Hard to get used to the Earthling lingo; even hot things are cool!) When I was chosen to be part of this team it was like a dream come true. But, of course, we don't dream over here.

Having been on the job for a while—a few years in earth time—I am getting bored. (We play Bahá'í Trivial Pursuit to kill time.) There are hosts of us waiting to help you folks with your teaching work. Since the Universal House of Justice placed great emphasis on Entry by Troops our department is upsizing by leaps and bounds. But we have not been getting calls for help as much as we expected. Sometimes we fight over calls. Fighting is not allowed here, but I learned how to be a bit aggressive from my earthling colleagues.

One day, hovering over the Shrine of The Báb, I had a few minutes to spare while the members of the House of Justice were having a lunch break. I decided to look around for exciting ideas on earth. I came across *Teach the Bahá'í Faith With Ease*. I thought "what a wonderful idea."

Let me tell you a bit about it. It deals with many aspects of promoting the Faith. You earthlings have to get really excited about teaching—the way we do. It is the most important work you can do during your days on Earth; Chapter One discusses this. The rest of the book will give you many tools and ideas about how to participate in this great task.

This books draws a lot from *Gleanings from the Writings of Bahá'u'lláh*, *Tablets from The Báb*, *Tablets of the Divine Plan*. These are excellent works, which I had to study as part of my preparation courses. You will also find the stories of how many became Bahá'ís very inspiring.

This book will help in your teaching work, and will create some activity over here for us. I hope you will call upon me, or any Earthling that you know who is on this side. We are waiting to serve you at any time. This is a promise of Bahá'u'lláh and it is in my job description. I know you can't see us, but we understand all your teaching problems and needs very well. If you yell for help, we'll make our presence known to you. It's a deal.

Yágnü
Crimson Ark Garden
Concourse on High

Splendor, 154, B.E.

# Preface

Man is the supreme Talisman... The Great Being saith:
Regard man as a mine rich in gems of inestimable value.
Education can, alone, cause it to reveal its treasures,
and enable mankind to benefit therefrom.

**Bahá'u'lláh**

## The Perpetual Revelation

A long time ago, God promised Abraham, a Prophet of the Old Testament, that He would never leave man alone. There would always be guidance from Him to His creatures. He would send One to be the Mouthpiece to reveal the knowledge of God. These chosen Ones are known as Prophets or Messengers of God. This is the eternal Covenant of God with Man. We know that there have been many Prophets, such as Moses, Krishna, Buddha, Zoroaster, Jesus, Muhammad, The Báb, and Bahá'u'lláh. Historically, many of these Prophets are descendants of Abraham. The guidance through these Holy Ones will always continue. As has happened in the past, their spirit comes back as the Messiah, the "return" or Avatar.

# Why this Revelation?

The latest Avatar or Prophet on this earth is Bahá'u'lláh, the Glory of God. He lived on this plane about hundred years ago to fulfil God's promise to Abraham. As in the past, He delivered God's Message, appropriate for this age. He revealed all the spiritual and social teachings needed for mankind till the next Prophet comes.

# Why Me, God?

When I joined the Faith, I made a promise not to share it with anyone else, or at least not to have discussions at firesides with the hope of converting someone. I thought it was preaching and preaching was just not my cup of tea. Somehow, over the years, I changed my mind.

Now, sharing the Message of Bahá'u'lláh is the most exhilarating experience in my Bahá'í life. No, I don't have great success in enrolling souls in the Faith, as many are so skillful at doing. But it seems every time I make an effort, regardless of the result, to acquaint someone with Bahá'u'lláh's Divine Message of the day, it is always uplifting and an enjoyable experience. I hope you will have the same experience.

# Why this Book?

For many years, I yearned for a book with all the information commonly used by teachers of the Faith. I know others would like to have the same; therefore, I wrote *Teach the Bahá'í Faith With Ease.*

# About This Book

The main purpose of this book is to inspire the reader to teach the Faith. Given the broad range of readers and unique ways each one is moved to teach, this is a major challenge. I consider this an attempt to meet the challenge, if only a beginning.

The approach taken when writing this book was to first answer some basic questions, like "Why does one have to teach?", "What are the benefits?", and "Is teaching the Faith important?" Next, we will examine the life of `Abdu'l-Bahá, our Hero and Exemplar. Throughout the book there are extracts from the charter of teaching, *Tablets of the Divine Plan*, full of hints to improve our teaching work. Finally, the book contains some inspiring stories of how many have found and joined the Bahá'í Faith.

This may also be used as a handbook. It is like a tool chest, full of useful information that one can use for teaching activities.

# Is This Book for You?

Potentially, this book is for every Bahá'í. The teaching work, so vital in the development of the Faith, is broken down into small, manageable pieces, each related to a different area of our lives where we have opportunities to teach. This book also addresses many concerns and inadequacies—often unvoiced—that many Bahá'ís have about teaching the Faith.

If you are new to the Faith, it will acquaint you with the requests and promises of Bahá'u'lláh about propagating His message, a message that accentuates so many fundamental truths. It will also give you cosmic reasons to be part of an ever-changing creation of God.

If you are hesitant about talking about religion because it makes you feel like a preacher, this book explores Bahá'u'lláh's request to His followers to share His precious Message with others.

If you are an ardent teacher of the Faith, this book might give you new and fresh ideas that you may not have thought of. Or you might want to use it as a reference. It will also give you the opportunity to measure your own teaching experience against the guidance presented in the following pages.

# A Word About Words

On every subject an attempt is made to give quotations from authoritative sources from The Báb, Bahá'u'lláh, 'Abdu'l-Bahá, Shoghi Effendi and the Universal House of Justice. When reading, I ask that you consider them as the most important parts of this book. To emphasize this they are printed in a distinct font, for example,

> The earth is but one country and mankind its citizens
> (**Bahá'u'lláh**, *Tablet of Bahá'u'lláh*, p. 167)

You will also notice that some words are printed in bold to emphasize their importance, for example,

> Say, Teach ye the Cause of God, O people of Bahá, for God hath **prescribed unto everyone the duty of proclaiming His Message**, and regardeth it as the most meritorious of all deeds.
> (**Bahá'u'lláh**, *Gleanings from the Writings of Bahá'u'lláh*, p. 278)

The second most important part of the book is the stories of how people became Bahá'ís. Each one is unique and inspiring. They are included to remind us of the love and joy that fill our heart when we make the decision to align our minds and souls to the most up-to-date Revelation of God. Also, they are examples of how easy and rewarding teaching the Message of Bahá'u'lláh can be.

You may have noticed that the Bahá'í Writings often contain many big words. Not everyone knows their meaning. To get a good understanding of any passages with these uncommon words, you have to refer to a dictionary. Wherever appropriate, the meaning of words has been included throughout the book. The dictionary used is *American Oxford Dictionary*. If you are not satisfied with the explanation, use your own favorite dictionary.

# A Touch of Humor

Teaching is a very serious business. As you will see throughout the book, it is one of the main driving forces to change the world for the better. This book is written with a touch of humor, not to take away from the importance of teaching, but to take a pause once in a while.

# What are Those Icons?

Throughout the book, there are icons associated with different parts to quickly identify them. They are:

 Word checks

 Teaching moment

 Teaching break

# Feedback

It would be nice to hear from you so that next time we may improve the quality of this book. Send your comments, corrections, suggestions, and teaching stories to the Internet address: **mgopaul@UnityWorks.com**.

Visit us at our web site: **WWW.UnityWorks.com**.

# Acknowledgments

Many have made this book possible. As you read the following pages, your will see their dedication and love for Bahá'u'lláh.

First, I want to thank Reggie Newkirk who has been helpful since its inception. He has always shown great interest in this book. Whenever I saw him at the Feast, Holy Days and so on, he would inquire—always with a big smile and encouraging words—about its progress. Also, he has offered many ideas to improve the quality of the book.

Whenever I need quotes or an answer to a particular question, I always went to Maddie Wingett. She would dig up the Writings with **Refer** (a document software) or post queries on the Bahá'í discussion groups on the Internet. A great teacher of the Faith, she has also shared many of her stories. Many thanks to Maddie.

I am indebted to Pat Verge for not only making sure the grammar and spelling are correct, but ensuring that every quotation comes from an authentic source. Also, she contributed many ideas that enhanced the quality of the book.

Many thanks to everyone who contributed their teaching stories. They are very important parts of this book.

Many thanks to Evan Long. When I requested the cartoons for this book, without any hesitation and in a short time, he drew about twenty of them. They were all very good. Unfortunately, due to lack of space only seven were used.

Finally, my special gratitude to my wife, Gaye; my daughter, Laila; and my son, Sanjiv, for their unfailing support and encouragement throughout this project; also for their understanding when I took time away from them.

V. Mitra Gopaul
Newmarket, Ontario Canada
March, 1997

# 1

## Getting Started

### Should I Teach the Bahá'í Faith?

Joe Shy was very happy to have found the Bahá'í Faith. After joining this new-found religion—something he had been searching for a long time—he spent a lot of time with the Bahá'ís. He made many new friends, regularly attended the Feast, contributed to the Funds and he was always glowing with spiritual health and vigor. One day his friend, Jane Highspirit, invited him to join her on a teaching trip to a neighborhood town where a few Bahá'í folks wanted to establish a new Spiritual Assembly soon.

At this request, he paused for a moment and politely declined the invitation; he could not make himself go on a teaching trip. He had never felt comfortable preaching; changing someone else's life was not his kind of thing to do. This made him think a lot about his role in sharing the message of Bahá'u'lláh with others.

Jane and Joe are fictional characters, but many of us share their feelings—Joe's hesitation and Jane's eagerness—when it comes to sharing the Faith. Traces of reluctance to share the message do not seem to vanish as we grow older as Bahá'ís. Talking about the Faith does not happen as freely as we would like. Consequently, a sense of frustration develops for having missed opportunities. But when we look at these feelings carefully, given our upbringing, these feelings are hard to avoid.

*How many of us grow up knowing how to teach our Faith?* Very few. Generally, we are more preoccupied in our teen and adolescent years with other things such as getting an education or training in anticipation of a career or just thinking of how to cope with living. To guide others spiritually is rarely one's goal in life. Even becoming a Bahá'í is unexpected, except for those who are raised in a Bahá'í family. Having to share the message of a new religion is rarely part of our life's preparation. Frustration and anxiety can easily set in, and if we are uncomfortable teaching, it should not be a surprise. Apart from looking at our inhibitions, to be a Bahá'í teacher also requires some skill.

Historically, an elite group has been responsible for the functions of protection and propagation in past religions. They take formal education and dedicate their whole lives to these duties. In Christianity this work is done by the clergy, by mulláhs in Islam, by swamis in Hinduism and by rabbis in Judaism.

But Bahá'u'lláh made dramatic changes in the history of religion. He not only abolished the long-revered institution of the clergy, but gave the responsibility of enlightening souls to every believer.

Now, let's look at the Bahá'í approach to attracting new adherents to its fold. Let's examine the plan of the Central Figures of the Faith to take their new-born religion to the world.

Bahá'u'lláh said:

> Say, Teach ye the Cause of God, O people of Bahá, for God hath **prescribed unto everyone the duty of proclaiming His Message**, and regardeth it as the most meritorious of all deeds.
>    (**Bahá'u'lláh**, *Gleanings from the Writings of Bahá'u'lláh*, p. 278)

This is the day in which to speak. It is **incumbent**

**upon the people of Bahá** to strive, with the utmost patience and forbearance, **to guide the peoples of the world to the Most Great Horizon.**

(**Shoghi Effendi**, *The Advent of Divine Justice*, pp. 82-83)

 WORD CHECK

| prescribe | 1. to advise the use of (a medicine, etc.)<br>2. to lay down as a course or rule to be followed |
|---|---|
| duty | 1. a moral or legal obligation<br>2. a task that must be done, action required from a particular person |
| meritorious | 1. having merit, deserving praise |
| incumbent | 1. forming an obligation or duty, *it is incumbent on you to warn people of the danger.* |
| patience | 1. calm endurance of hardship or annoyance or inconvenience or delay, etc.<br>2. perseverance |
| forbearance | 1. patience<br>2. tolerance |

Traditionally, clergy of all religions enjoyed a privileged position as they were among the very few who received any education. They guided the illiterate masses socially and spiritually. In this age, however, education is gradually becoming universal and for the first time in history the masses are able to read the Holy Writings for themselves, allowing them to take the responsibility of their spiritual destiny into their own hands.

It is an irony that the ecclesiastics lost spiritual insight and failed to recognize the new religion of The Báb and Bahá'u'lláh. In fact, they were the main force of opposition to it. Bahá'u'lláh eliminated the clerical system and placed the duty of propagation of the Faith directly before every Bahá'í. We call it teaching the Bahá'í Faith, which simply means sharing it with others in the hope that they will show some interest and perhaps join it.

From Bahá'u'lláh's instructions, it is very clear that God is asking His beloved followers to expand His Cause. Every time God makes a request, He showers us with countless rewards. The All-Mighty, All-Knowing and All-Powerful God, who also emanates other superlative qualities, does not really depend on our time, money or efforts. He is totally independent of His creation. In fact, everything in the whole of creation comes from Him. With a single stroke of a pen, He can convert every single soul to the Bahá'í Faith; He can build thousands of temples around the world; He can establish the World Order; and He can bring in the Most Great Peace. He can do all of them in a twinkling of an eye. But this is not His design.

*Why does He ask us to do anything for Him?* Simple. He wants us to be part of the creative processes of the universe. Here, on earth, the divine goal is to build a New World Order, which will bring about the Golden Age of humankind. God wants us to participate in this renewal of human existence and if we choose to voluntarily abide by His wishes, the benefits are endless.

## Wishful Thinking

Joe Shy, after some thought, decided to share the good news with others. He changed his name to Joe Pioneer and married Jane Highspirit. Both pioneered to Paradise Island in the Pacific Ocean. After teaching the Bahá'í Faith to everyone on this beautiful place, both died and lived ever after in the Abhá Kingdom.

# Teaching and Knowledge of God

When we survey Bahá'u'lláh's Writings, we can classify His instructions to us into three different categories. The first kind talks about the actions that directly benefit us, for example, prayer, fasting, refraining from alcohol and so on.

The second type of duty benefits the society we live in. Our individual actions affect the well-being of others with whom we come in contact. These society-changing agents are divine attributes, such as love, patience, kindness, and so on, that are shown to others.

The third category of request asks us to do something for His Cause; it is like God asking us to do a job for Him. One such request is to help others know more about the nature of God through the Divine Message of the most recent Manifestation. Another such duty is giving to the Bahá'í Funds.

Let's look a bit closer at the third category. It is the most astonishing request. It comes from God, who is the All-Mighty, the Creator of the universe, Who with just a single Word, can make every single living creature on this planet bow down before Him. He can make every soul a believer in Bahá'u'lláh. However, this is not the way He wants His creatures to get closer to Him. Rather, human beings are to discover the Creator according to his or her own volition, without any pressure. Bahá'ís have been chosen to help in this process.

When it comes to doing God's work, it is important to always remember that He does not really need us. He is All-Knowing, Everlasting, All-Powerful, and independent of His creation. He can make all His wishes come true and promises happen without a helping hand from any one of us.

But God being God—One who can make any wish come true—makes this unique and incomparable request, and offers incredible benefits which we will look at shortly. Always remember that teaching the Faith is not subject to administrative sanctions, you will not be expelled from the Faith or lose administrative rights if you do not teach; however, it is a profound obligation. Because the rewards are so great, in spite of lack of training or skills, every Bahá'í should seriously consider becoming a teacher.

*Why?* Talking about the Bahá'í Faith to one who is not a Bahá'í is not a very difficult job compared to hundreds of tasks we perform in our life time; yet it is the most unique. By doing it, the teacher makes the Creator known a bit more. It is not a surprise that it is the most important work. This ties in with the purpose of creation itself stated in the daily obligatory prayer:

> I bear witness, O my God, that thou hast created me
> to know Thee and to worship Thee.
> **(Bahá'u'lláh**, *Bahá'í Prayers*, p.4)

In the world of Islam, there is a very well-known tradition:

> I was a Hidden Treasure and loved to be known.
> Therefore, I created the Creation that I might be
> known.
> **(Balyuzi, H. M.**, *'Abdu'l-Bahá*, p. 14)

These two quotations give in a simple but clear way the reason for God to bring the whole universe—including us Earthlings—into existence so He can become known by His own creatures.

# How Generous are the Benefits?

For teaching the Cause of God, you may ask, "What do I really get?"  A fair question. In this divine deal we want to know what each party gets.  From God's side, He gets to be more known among His creatures. According to The Báb, Bahá'u'lláh, and 'Abdu'l-Bahá, the teacher gets these rewards:

> It is better to guide one soul than to possess all
> that is on earth, for as long as that guided soul

is under the shadow of the Tree of Divine Unity, he and the one who hath guided him will both **be recipients of God's tender mercy**, whereas possession of earthly things will cease at the time of death.

    (**The Báb**, *Selections from the Writings of The Báb*, p. 77)

Indeed if thou dost open the heart of a person for His sake, **better will it be for thee than every virtuous deed**; since deeds are secondary to faith in Him...

    (**The Báb**, *Selections from the Writings of The Báb*, p. 77)

The **source of courage and power** is the promotion of the Word of God, and steadfastness in His Love.

    (**Bahá'u'lláh**, *Tablets of Bahá'u'lláh*, p. 156)

Should you be aided to render such a service, rest ye assured that your **heads shall be crowned with the diadem of everlasting sovereignty**, and at the threshold of oneness you will **become the favored and accepted servants**.

    ('**Abdu'l-Bahá**, *Tablets of the Divine Plan*, revealed on April 8, 1916, p. 10)

Of all the gifts of God the greatest is the gift of Teaching. It draweth unto us **the Grace of God** and is our first obligation.

    ('**Abdu'l-Bahá**, *The Will and Testament of 'Abdu'l-Bahá*, p. 25)

Become thou engaged in teaching the truth, for teaching of the Cause containeth **the power of a magnet**; it **attracteth the mysteries of God**.

    ('**Abdu'l-Bahá**, *Tablets of 'Abdu'l-Bahá*, p. 225)

And now you, if you act in accordance with the teachings of Bahá'u'lláh, may rest assured that you will **be aided and confirmed**. In all affairs you undertake, you will **be rendered victorious**, and all the inhabitants of the earth cannot withstand you...
    (**'Abdu'l-Bahá**, *Star of the West*, Vol. VIII, p.103)

Today the greatest of all divine bestowals is teaching the Cause of God for it is **fraught with confirmations**. Every teacher is **confirmed** and is **favored at the Divine Threshold**.
    (**Shoghi Effendi**, *Japan Will Turn Ablaze*, p. 12)

He that hath acknowledged this principle will be **endowed with the most perfect constancy**. All honor to this all-glorious station, the remembrance of which adorneth every exalted Tablet. Such is the teaching which will **deliver you from all manner of doubt and perplexity**, and **enable you to attain unto salvation in both this world and in the next**. He, verily, is the Ever-Forgiving, the Most Bountiful.
    (**Bahá'u'lláh**, *Gleanings from the Writings of Bahá'u'lláh*, p. 37)

The benefits are so important and great that you would want to frame this list and place it where you can see or read it every day. It is something you want to remember for the rest of your life. Here are the benefits:

- be recipients of God's tender mercy
- better will it be for thee than every virtuous deed
- source of courage and power
- heads shall be crowned with the diadem of everlasting sovereignty
- become the favored and accepted servants
- attract the Grace of God

- the power of a magnet
- attract the mysteries of God
- be aided and confirmed
- be rendered victorious
- fraught with confirmations
- confirmed and favored at the Divine Threshold
- the most perfect constancy
- deliver you from all manner of doubt and perplexity
- enable you to attain unto salvation in both this world and in the next

## WORD CHECK

| | |
|---|---|
| **mercy** | **refraining from inflicting punishment or pain on an offender or enemy, etc., who is in one's power** |
| **virtuous** | having or showing moral virtue |
| **courage** | to be brave enough to do what one feels to be right |
| **power** | vigor, energy, strength |
| **diadem** | 1. a crown or headband worn as a sign of sovereignty. <br> 2. royal authority or status, *the diadem has passed to the younger son.* |
| **sovereign** | 1. supreme power. <br> 2. possessing sovereign power, independent. <br> 3. very effective. |
| **grace** | 1. God's free and undeserved favor to and love for mankind; the influence of God operating in man to improve or strengthen him. <br> 2. the condition of being influenced and favored by God. |
| **mysteries** | 1. a matter that remains unexplained or secret. <br> 2. a religious truth that is beyond human powers to understand |
| **fraught** | filled, involving, *fraught with danger.* |

# A Mighty Task

There are 5 million Bahá'ís around the world and there are 5.5 billion who need to hear Bahá'u'lláh's message. This Faith is for everyone. Every soul on this planet must be given a chance to hear about it. Just looking at these numbers makes the task seem like a mighty one. But we have to do it sooner or later. There is no avoiding it in the long run. God has already made big promises, like World Peace, World Order, the Golden Age. These future events will happen whether you or I participate or not. God is not going to break a promise.

Perhaps you live in a city with a population of 5 million and there are 1,000 Bahá'ís. The job of giving the message is indeed huge.

# Divine Help and Support

Now, God knows that taking Bahá'u'lláh's message to the entire world population would not be a trivial undertaking. He also knows that in spite of all the attractive incentives, Bahá'ís would not be able to accomplish this mighty task alone. In the equation of teaching there is another very important and essential part: an array of help from both existences, heaven and earth, are placed in front of teachers. Let's look at the help available.

## *Central Figures*

We have the Writings of the Báb and Bahá'u'lláh, which give us instructions on teaching. These Words, coming directly from God, are sources of potent inspiration that will motivate us to share the most recent Divine Message. During Their ministries, both the Báb and Bahá'u'lláh played direct roles in propagating this new religion during the crucial moments of the history of the Faith. Their involvement in the expansion is so vast that it could cover many volumes. The Báb and Bahá'u'lláh guided many illustrious teachers in their service.

During the Báb's short dispensation, among the most effective teachers were the Letters of the Living; He charged them to proclaim the new-born religion and acquaint their contacts with His revolutionary message. He inspired them with these weighty words:

> O My Letters! Verily I say, immensely exalted is this Day above the days of the Apostles of old. Nay, immeasurable is the difference! You are the witnesses of the Dawn of the promised Day of God. You are the partakers of the mystic chalice of His Revelation.
>
> Gird up the loins of endeavor, and be mindful of the words of God as revealed in His Book: 'Lo, the Lord thy God is come, and with Him is the company of His angels arrayed before Him!'
>    (**Balyuzi, H. M.**, *The Báb*, p. 29)

## The Perfect Example

Bahá'u'lláh also knew the kind of difficulty we would encounter in teaching His Cause. As the Great Architect of the Bahá'í Dispensation, He gave us His Son, 'Abdu'l-Bahá, the perfect exemplar. 'Abdu'l-Bahá fulfilled many roles in His life, but one of the most outstanding was as a teacher of the Bahá'í Faith. Through love, spirit and the Words of His Father, He inspired many souls to get closer to God.

He was an expert. As a human being, He understood exactly how to share the Bahá'í message. People of all kinds—poor, rich, learned, illiterate, powerful, meek—all received a share of Bahá'u'lláh's blessings, whether through deeds, love, or words. The next chapter is devoted to His teaching moments.

## Concourse on High

All the help mentioned so far should be enough to teach every soul on earth about the Bahá'í Cause. But no. There is more. Like waiters/waitresses in a restaurant, holy souls from the spiritual world are just waiting to take our orders. All we have to do is make our needs known and help will rush to us. Both Bahá'u'lláh and 'Abdu'l-Bahá attest to it through these words:

Whoso openeth his lips in this Day and maketh mention of the name of his Lord, the hosts of Divine inspiration shall descend upon him from the heaven of My name, the All-Knowing, the All-Wise. On him shall also descend the Concourse on high, each bearing aloft a chalice of pure light.

(**Bahá'u'lláh**, *Gleanings from the Writings of Bahá'u'lláh*, p. 280)

However, when the tongue of the teacher is engaged in teaching, he will naturally himself be stimulated, will become a magnet attracting the divine aid and bounty of the Kingdom, and will be like unto the bird at the hour of dawn, which itself becometh exhilarated by its own singing, its warbling and its melody.

('**Abdu'l-Bahá**, *The Individual and Teaching*, p. 10)

The teacher, when teaching, must be himself fully enkindled, so that his utterance, like  unto a flame , may exert influence and consume the veil of self and passion. He must also be utterly humble and lowly, so that others may be edified and be totally self-effaced and evanescent so that he may teach with the melody of the Concourse on high—otherwise his teaching will have no effect.

('**Abdu'l-Bahá**, *The Individual and Teaching*, p. 10)

Again, we should not hesitate in asking for help. All we have to do is ask—assistance will come, freely.

 **Word Check**

| exhilarate | to make very happy or lively. |
|---|---|
| enkindle | to arouse or stimulate. |
| edify | to be an uplifting influence on the mind of a person. |
| evanescent | fading quickly. |

## The Guardianship

One of the greatest achievements of Shoghi Effendi, the Guardian of the Bahá'í Faith, was establishing the foundation of the Bahá'í institutions. He accomplished this by mobilizing many pioneers throughout the world. They left their homes and went to far and near places to attract searching souls to the Faith. Encouraging the Bahá'ís to teach the Faith was a very vital part of Shoghi Effendi's own mission. His writings are a vital source of guidance for individual Bahá'ís and institutions in the arena of teaching.

He had a very unique position. Although not a prophet himself, the Bahá'ís were assured in the *Will and Testament of 'Abdu'l-Bahá* that Shoghi Effendi would be infallibly guided in the matters belonging to the Faith. Here are some thoughts of Shoghi Effendi on teaching:

The harder you strive to attain your goal, the greater will be the confirmations of Bahá'u'lláh, and the more certain you can feel to attain

success. Be cheerful, therefore, and exert
yourself with faith and confidence. For
Bahá'u'lláh has promised His Divine assistance to
everyone who arises with a pure and detached heart
to spread His holy Word, even though he may be
bereft of every human knowledge and capacity, and
notwithstanding the forces of darkness and
opposition which may be arrayed against him.

   (**Shoghi Effendi**, *From a letter dated 3 February 1937 written to an individual believer*)

## The Universal House of Justice

Since the passing of Shoghi Effendi, infallible guidance continues through the Universal House of Justice. When we receive messages and plans from this supreme institution and head of the Faith, expansion is always central. Through the help of other institutions, namely, the International Teaching Center and the Continental Board of Counsellors, the Universal House of Justice guides us, from the Bahá'í World Center, Haifa, Israel, in the teaching work throughout the world. Authoritative and infallible guidance is reaching all corners of the globe, daily. This is new in the history of mankind.

On 22 July 1980, the Universal House of Justice reminded us, through a letter written to all National Spiritual Assemblies, of the priority of teaching:

The teaching work, both that organized by
institutions of the Faith and that which is the
fruit of individual initiative, must be actively
carried forward so that there will be growing
numbers of believers, leading more countries to
the stage of entry by troops and ultimately to
mass conversion.

### Other Institutions

Closer to home, there are other institutions, such as National and Local Spiritual Assemblies and Auxiliary Board members and their assistants, which are designed to promote the Cause of God. Although they are not infallible, they follow closely the guidance of the Universal House of Justice. One of their main functions is to support the individual Bahá'ís in their teaching work. This is done in many different ways, for example:

- Encourage teaching of individuals
- Formulate, execute, and evaluate plans
- Provide material and in some cases financial resources to those who arise to teach
- Pray for the success of teaching efforts
- Provide for teacher training programs

In conclusion, help in the arena of teaching comes in many forms and from many directions.

 TEACHING MOMENT—MYSTERIOUS

WAVES

"When we were in Belize City [Belize] in a suburb, I think it was called Jamestown, but more commonly referred to as Trench Town. It was very poor, kind of almost a shanty town of refugee people, migrant people who moved into Belize City, built their own little house, were kind of trying to make a living. There was a lady, kind of a funny lady, with a loud voice and good sense of humor. We had visited her and she said, 'look, I can't really, I don't really have the time right now. Why don't you come back at another time?' And she gave us a time. So we came back at the time that she had said, and apparently that wasn't a good time, either. She said, 'no, I've got things to do and I can't really take the time now, come back on Sunday.' So we went back Sunday in the late morning, early afternoon. So, by this time, I came by myself, there was no-one else to travel with me.

So I went over to this lady's house. And I went in, and her mood had changed, and she said, 'you know, I'm sorry I wasted your time, I'm really not interested. My husband's here and we have a faith, a belief and I'm sorry, I'm not interested.' And they kind of lived in a row housing, like a town house. Next door, it looked like kind of a party was going on. A bunch of young people, there were some kids. So I went across into their backyard and I went to the door and I said, 'look, I'm a Bahá'í, I was in the neighborhood, I'd like to teach the Bahá'í Faith, if anybody here is interested.' And generally, they said well, they weren't interested and I'd better leave. So I turned around to leave and there were some wires, like telephone wires behind their house in the alley. And I was about to cross the yard and go through the alley and these wires started to undulate, kind of like gentle waves. And soon these waves became more dramatic and more pronounced, and there was maybe like six wires. And some of these wires became really big, big, it's like if you took a whip and you went at one end and this big curve would run all the way down to the end and then it would run all the way back. And then this waving motion became so violent, that one of the wires broke. And then every time it would touch something, it would flash sparks, it would hit the post, it would hit the road, it would hit other wires.

And then another wire broke and soon all of the wires were wildly waving. And by this time, people in both the houses came out. And these wires, literally every single wire broke and just showered sparks around. Everyone stood motionless looking at this sight. And then it stopped. Suddenly, it stopped, all the wires went dead. And then there was a voice in the room of the house that I'd just been in, 'hey, maybe we should invite that white man in to talk about God.' And they invited me in to the house--'what was it that you were going to tell us?' And there was a couple of people that were kind of drunk and these couple of people said,'no, we don't want to hear about God.' But the whole room just shouted them down and said, 'listen to the man, he's got a message from God!'

A couple of people took cards, but I am not sure that they ever declared themselves as Bahá'ís. But it was a group of people that really hung on to every word that I said!"

**Ted Glabush,** Calgary, Alberta, Canada

# What is the Minimum Requirement?

After carefully examining the concept to make God known among His creatures and the rewards that come with it, you may ask how difficult it is to teach the Bahá'í Faith. When enrolling in the Faith, no one gives us a teaching manual, nor is there often formal training to become teachers of the Faith. At first you may feel awkward and uncomfortable even trying it.

Actually, teaching the Bahá'í Faith, as we will see shortly, is one of the easiest tasks you can do, compared to many other things we do in life. It is easier and the rewards are greater, than, say, raising children, earning a living, fighting spiritual battles, studying at university and so on. At most, it may just require some of your time, without any risk at all, in exchange for benefits that are incomparable.

You may wonder if there is a sure-fire technique or method that you can deploy. Unfortunately, there is no one method you can apply to all situations. The way you would teach in Rio de Janeiro, Brazil, may be different from Québec, Canada. Even in your own community, the approach may vary from one person to another. The best approach is to try a few teaching sessions with the hope of developing a number of methods that work for you. By practicing, the effectiveness of each will gradually improve.

Methods and techniques may vary from one person to another or from one country to another. The minimum requirement for teaching the Faith is explained by

Bahá'u'lláh with these words:

> O Friends! You must all be so ablaze in this day
> with the fire of the **love of God** that the heat
> thereof may be manifest in all your veins, your
> limbs and members of your body, and the peoples of
> the world may be ignited by this heat and turn to
> the horizon of the Beloved.
>    (**Bahá'u'lláh**, *The Individual and Teaching*, p. 3)

To promote the knowledge of God, one has to have the love of God first.

It is important to ponder for a moment on the love of God in your heart. Every Bahá'í has it. Sometimes we may not show it, but, deep inside, it exists. It is the main ingredient that attracted us to the Faith and the one that keeps us within it.

We are always thankful to the one that kindled our soul with the light of Bahá'u'lláh. Bahá'ís are like lit candles around the world. When we teach effectively, we are trying to enkindle the candle of other souls with the same light. Someday everyone on this planet will burn with the same love of God.

Teaching the Faith is a life-time—not necessarily full-time—duty. Like anything we do, we will make mistakes and hopefully learn how to avoid them the next time. If we improve consistently, we will sharpen our skills, making the teaching work more effective. In the following chapters, we will look at some of the ways of improving those skills.

A busy life does sometimes take a toll. Often, it leaves us spiritually depleted at the end of the day. It may put us in a lethargic state for a while and, consequently, we may not feel like teaching. To get back on our "spiritual feet," we need to replenish ourselves with some spirit. One of many ways to do this is to meditate on the love of God that once welled in our hearts when we joined the Faith. It is always there, deep down. Remembering those resplendent moments will certainly make us glow again.

# Primary Duty

In the spectrum of human experience, there are thousands of possible tasks. They range from being a mother to scientist, a member of a Local Spiritual Assembly to the Universal House of Justice, a carpenter to an artist, and so on.

*What is the most important task?* Teaching. In the sight of God, there is nothing better you can do in this life. Every other duty in all human experience is considered secondary. Here are some clarifications:

> Indeed if thou dost open the heart of a person for His sake, better will it **be for thee than every virtuous deed**; since deeds are secondary to faith in Him...
>    (**The Báb**, *Selections from the Writings of the Báb*, p. 77)

> The **greatest glory and honor** which can come to an individual is to bring the light of guidance to some new soul. The quickening power of the Holy Spirit, which has come into the world through Bahá'u'lláh, is the source of immortal life; and those who are quickened by this spirit in this world will find themselves in great honor and glory in the next world.
>    ('**Abdu'l-Bahá**, *The individual and Teaching*, p. 35)

> They that have forsaken their country for the purpose of teaching Our Cause—these shall the Faithful Spirit strengthen through its power. A company of Our chosen angels shall go forth with them, as bidden by Him Who is the Almighty, the All-Wise. How **great the blessedness** that awaiteth him that hath attained the honor of serving the Almighty! By My life! No act, however great, can

compare with it, except such deeds as have been
ordained by God, the All-Powerful, the Most Mighty.
Such a service is, indeed, the **prince of all goodly
deeds**, and the **ornament of every goodly act**. Thus
hath it been ordained by Him Who is the Sovereign
Revealer, the Ancient of Days.

   (**Bahá'u'lláh**, *Gleanings from the Writings of Bahá'u'lláh*, p. 334)

These superlative words emphasize the importance of teaching the Bahá'í
Faith—that it is our primary work according to God. Thus, it becomes evident
why God is so generous when one volunteers to make Him known.

One might argue that humans see things differently from God. This happens all
the time. From an individual's perspective, teaching may not be the most
important task. It could be many other things, like serving on Bahá'í institutions,
raising a family, pursuing a career or finding a cure for cancer. We have been
given free will, and no one takes it away from us, including the All-Mighty God.
We are free to prioritize our life in whatever ways we want.

But it is worth reconsidering teaching and placing it at the top of the priority list,
given the far-reaching implications. The interesting part of this task is that it is
one of the easiest you can do. It brings less anxiety than raising a family; less
frustration than serving the administration; less fatigue than daily career work. It
can be more spiritually rejuvenating than all of them. All you have to do is convey
the Bahá'í message—you are already familiar with it—to a listener and you are
not even responsible for how the listener receives it.

Obviously, the request to make God known is an open offer to any Bahá'í. Like
many aspects of the Faith, except the compulsory ones, you don't have to do it if
you don't want. No teaching cop is going to check up on you! But, before you
decline, you should carefully consider the great rewards that are promised in
exchange for so little effort.

Without breathing, a body will be starved of oxygen and die. Fortunately, the
mechanism of the body is such that breathing happens automatically. The

essential supply of oxygen is not interrupted during waking or sleeping moments. Unlike breathing, teaching does not happen automatically.

With our busy lives, inviting a neighbor to a fireside, dropping a pamphlet at our child's school or mentioning a principle to a colleague can be put aside. One does have to make a conscientious effort to ensure the teaching work is happening all the time.

# Spiritual Motherhood

Ever since humans have been born, no one has come to this planet with an operating manual. From generation to generation, mothers have managed to take care of the newly-born and raise them in an ever-progressing civilization. Through the ages, there have been all kinds of mothers: educated, illiterate, too young, too old, heathy, sick and so on. In spite of many differing capacities, there are two things that are common to most, if not all. They are love and instinct.

Giving birth and raising a human being is one of the most difficult, complicated, and demanding tasks on this planet. Mothers have to learn on the job. The urgency to learn is so great that after the first child, many become experts, or, at least, master child-raising to a high degree. Mothers do make mistakes—they are the first to admit it—but most of them do not turn away from their mothering responsibilities. Each develops a unique approach to handling daily situations. Each mother makes adjustments to suit the needs of each child. Most often, they raise more than one child at a time. In spite of all the sacrifices that mothers have to make, they reap the reward of feeling proud of raising another human being.

Teaching the Bahá'í Faith to someone is like witnessing the second birth of a soul. It has many similarities to physical birth. Like motherhood, one must be flexible, and adjust to the needs of individual souls. There is no one universal method that will satisfy the needs of every soul on this planet. We are made up of our personal experience, cultural influences, and racial background. In addition, we have different growth levels. When all these variations are combined together, it makes the spiritual requirements of every soul unique; therefore, each gets closer to God in a special way. Like motherhood, there are two things that are needed in a teaching experience. They are love and common sense.

# TEACHING MOMENT—SPIRITUAL MOTHER

During the time that I operated my beauty salon I was introduced to a young girl named Carole Dixon (now Cummings). She was only in her teens at that time and was having a few difficulties in her life as all teens do at one time or another. The young girl who assisted me in my shop asked me if I would talk to her. I knew many teenagers in Lakefield, Ontario, and was trying to mother them all. She was having problems with her boyfriend at the time and I tried to explain to her about the spiritual side of a relationship and that I knew this from the Bahá'í teachings.

Well, being the bright girl that she is, she asked me what was the Bahá'í Faith. During the next six years, we had many discussions. She would call me to her home at least twice a week and I would hardly have my coat off when she was asking me again to prove to her the truth of Bahá'u'lláh's claim. I was so stunned the day she finally declared that I could hardly believe my ears. I had to ask her several times if she was sure she really believed and understood who Bahá'u'lláh was. She had come up with so many reasons not to believe that when she decided to accept the Faith, it seemed incredible. After asking Carole so many times, with tears running down my face, she said, "Well, maybe I better think about it for a while longer." I thought I lost her. But she rallied around and the next day, she signed her declaration card.

Through her own teaching efforts, her mother, two sisters, and two aunts became Bahá'ís.

**Maddie Wingett**, Peterborough, Ontario, Canada

# The Apostles

*Have you ever thought of yourself as an apostle?* Have you ever thought of being in the same league as the twelve disciples of Christ or the Letters of the Living of the Bábí Dispensation? If you have not, consider this definition from 'Abdu'l-Bahá:

O ye apostles of Bahá'u'lláh—May my life be sacrificed for you!

The blessed Person of the Promised One is interpreted in the Holy Book as the Lord of Hosts—the heavenly armies. By heavenly armies those souls are intended who are entirely freed from the human world, transformed into celestial spirits and have become divine angels. Such souls are the rays of the Sun of Reality who will illumine all the continents. Each one is holding in his hand a trumpet, blowing the breath of life over all the regions. They are delivered from human qualities and the defects of the world of nature, are characterized with the characteristics of God, and are attracted with the fragrances of the Merciful. Like unto the apostles of Christ, who were filled with Him, these souls have also become filled with His Holiness Bahá'u'lláh; that is, the love of Bahá'u'lláh has so mastered every organ, part and limb of their bodies, as to leave no effect from the promptings of the human world.

These souls are the armies of God and the conquerors of the East and the West. Should one of them turn his face toward some direction and summon the people to the Kingdom of God, all the ideal forces and lordly confirmations will rush to his support and reinforcement. He will behold all the doors open and all the strong fortifications and impregnable castles razed to the ground. Singly and alone he will attack the armies of the world, defeat the right and left wings of the hosts of all the countries, break through the lines of the legions of all the nations and carry his attack to the very center of the powers of the earth. This is the meaning of the Hosts of God.

Any soul from among the believers of Bahá'u'lláh who attains to this station, will become known as the Apostle of Bahá'u'lláh.

('**Abdu'l-Bahá**, *Tablets of the Divine Plan*, revealed on April 19, 20, and 22, 1916, p. 17)

 WORD CHECK

| apostle | 1. any of the twelve men sent forth by Jesus to preach the Gospel. 2. a leader or teacher of a new faith or movement. |
| --- | --- |

# Summary

To make God known to His creatures is an important request that deserves very serious consideration by each of Bahá'u'lláh's followers. The implications of this—our primary duty on this physical plane—are far-reaching and beyond one's imagination. For the individual, teaching will attract incomparable bounties enjoyable both on earth and in the other worlds of God. A Bahá'í teacher also participates in the fulfillment of God's promises to humanity: The Most Great Peace, the World Order of Bahá'u'lláh, and the Golden Age of mankind.

There are many barriers that prevent us from disseminating the Faith the way we could. Some of them are:

- Fear and hesitation
- Lack of understanding
- Too busy at work
- Too busy with Bahá'í administrative responsibilities
- Too busy with raising children
- Too occupied with family
- Fatigue

One of the ways to make all of them evaporate is to think about the benefits, which we saw earlier:

- be recipients of God's tender mercy and grace
- better will it be for thee than every virtuous deed
- source of courage and power
- heads shall be crowned with the diadem of everlasting sovereignty
- become the favored and accepted servants
- the benefit to the teacher in growth is as ninety percent
- the Grace of God
- the power of a magnet
- attract the mysteries of God
- be aided and confirmed

- be rendered victorious
- fraught with confirmations
- confirmed and favored at the Divine Threshold
- the most perfect constancy
- deliver you from all manner of doubt and perplexity
- enable you to attain unto salvation in both this world and in the next

'Abdu'l-Bahá summarized the importance of this day in this way:

> The holy realities of the Concourse on High, yearn,
> in this day, in the Most Exalted Paradise, to
> return unto this world, so that they may be aided
> to render some service to the threshold of the Abhá
> Beauty, and arise to demonstrate their service to
> His threshold.
>
> (**Shoghi Effendi**, *Guidance for Today and Tomorrow*, Chapter XII)

The rest of the book is devoted to making this important work easier and more effective.

# TEACHING BREAK

# 2

## 'Abdu'l-Bahá: The Perfect Exemplar

In the last chapter, we looked at the enormous bounty of being able to share the divine message for this day and promote God's Cause. We also discovered that an unprecedented and generous outpouring of grace comes to those who participate in this cosmic event of making God known to His creatures, a process linked to the purpose of creation itself. To fulfil this task, God has placed many things at our disposal. He not only gives us generous benefits and support as ways to motivate us to teach, but He did something even more special in this Revelation. He gave us a perfect living exemplar of how to teach the Bahá'í Faith.

The Exemplar of course is 'Abdu'l-Bahá. This divine gift is so far-reaching and unique—at least in the history of humankind—that all its various aspects cannot be sufficiently explored in a single chapter. Here, we will briefly look at some of the teaching activities in the life of 'Abdu'l-Bahá. Hopefully, they will inspire you to teach more and better.

## Why Do We Need 'Abdu'l-Bahá?

According to the Bahá'í Revelation, His existence is necessary at this time of human history. It is up to each one of us to benefit from this further bounty of our Faith.

One of the most fundamental aspects of learning is to imitate others. Children do this all the time. They look at adults for clues and cues for development and knowledge. Scientific experiments tell us that if a child were to grow up among animals, say, monkeys, the best this human being would do is to imitate all the monkey behaviors. As we grow, we look up to our parents, friends, teachers, and others in our midst for developing our character and skills. In some cases we admire other people, for example, politicians, writers, spiritual leaders, socialists, singers, athletes, sports players, movie stars and so on, with whom we can align our thoughts and behaviors. We acquire fondness and respect towards them as we value and admire them. Regardless of good or bad influence, we adopt them as our mentors. Looking up to a model is a natural part of our individual and collective growth and development. In fact, we are so fascinated by such outstanding characters in society that we are willing to make them our heroes. This is part of the human experience.

Spiritually, 'Abdu'l-Bahá is our Hero. His being has many facets. When it comes to teaching the Bahá'í Faith, He sets the standards, patterns and methods. We must study His life and work as we study many other human enterprises. If you want to be a great orator, you have to study the life and work of great orators. If you want to be an excellent singer, you have to know and understand great singers. The same applies to other fields, such as politics, science, art, and so on, including teaching the Bahá'í Faith.

Once Bahá'u'lláh was asked how to teach His Cause. He pointed to the Master as the example to follow. He paid special attention to 'Abdu'l-Bahá's technique and said:

```
Consider the way in which the Master teaches the
people. He listens very carefully to the most
hollow and senseless talk. He listens so intently
that the speaker says to himself,"He is trying to
learn from me." Then the Master gradually and very
```

```
carefully, by means that the other person does not
perceive, puts him on the right path and endows him
with a fresh power of understanding.
```
(**Faizi, A. Q.**, *Stories from the Delight of Hearts*, p. 110)

This instruction from the Prophet sounds like a very simple story, yet it demonstrates the most essential element of sharing the Faith with others. We will see later some of the most effective methods to teach which 'Abdu'l-Bahá used extensively to promote His Father's Cause.

## What's in a Name?

When 'Abdu'l-Bahá was born, He was named Abbas Effendi. During His youth and adult years, Bahá'u'lláh asked the believers to refer to His Son as the Master. However, after the passing of Bahá'u'lláh, He changed His own name to 'Abdu'l-Bahá, which means the Servant of Glory.

'Abdu'l-Bahá finds glory in being a servant, a notion so contrary to popular thinking. When we look closer at servitude, on this plane we all are servants. We earn the money by working for our employer. Our boss can afford our salary by selling a product or service to others. When we go to a store, someone serves us. We are all connected in this chain of servitude. Even the kings, queens, presidents, stars, and wealthy maintain their positions by offering some kind of service to society. As Bahá'ís, one of the greatest services we can render is to promote the Cause of God.

## Focus

Throughout His life, 'Abdu'l-Bahá was very focused. Every waking moment, He found opportunities to promote the Cause of His Father. Once He said:

```
Look at me. All my thoughts are centered around
```

proclamation of the Kingdom. I have a lamp in my hand searching through the lands and seas to find souls who can become heralds of the Cause. Day and night I am engaged in this work.

(**Motlagh, Hushidar**, *Teaching: The Crown of Immortal Glory*, p. iv)

 # Word Check

| heralds | a person indicating the approach of something |
|---------|-----------------------------------------------|
| engaged | occupied with |

# The Longing

As the servant of Bahá, 'Abdu'l-Bahá's greatest desire was to illumine the world with the light of God. Knowing the suffering of humanity, this was His ultimate goal. Before passing on to the spirit world, He expressed His longing in these words:

O that I could travel, even though on foot and in the utmost poverty...to promote the divine teachings!...Should you be aided to render such a service, rest ye assured that your heads shall be crowned with a **diadem** of everlasting sovereignty.

('**Abdu'l-Bahá**, *Tablets of the Divine Plan*, revealed on April 8, 1916, p. 10)

# Word Check

| promote | to initiate or help the progress of. |
|---------|--------------------------------------|
| render | to give, especially in return or exchange or as something due, *a reward for services rendered.* |

Unfortunately, time and circumstances were not in His favor to accomplish His cherished goal. But what He achieved in His lifetime was phenomenal.

 TEACHING MOMENT—WHAT IS THE PURPOSE OF LIFE?

It all started one summer in 1959 when I was sitting on the sand dunes near my village in Northumberland, England. I was in my 19th year, and had just completed another week of work underground, as a coal miner. It was one of those rare days for that part of the world, sunny and warm. As I sat there, I began thinking about the purpose of life. I could not believe my only reason for existence was to be born, go to this mine daily for the rest of my working life, then die. I reasoned without the benefit of an education because I left school just before my fifteenth birthday, without a spiritual upbringing, and without influence from friends or family, that there must be a higher purpose for being. It was intuitive. Having said this, I had no idea what to do about it, so there it was left.

One Sunday evening, a short time later, while discussing the evening plans with my friends—should we go to the movies, church, or the pub?—for some reason I considered that the plan of action was hypocritical. And to this day I do not know why. I only know that my intuition told me that I would one day find a religion that was not hypocritical in word or deed. My friends naturally greeted my ideals with a friendly sarcasm. However, I got my way and we went to the movies.

By 1964, I had been married with two children and immigrated to Hamilton, Ontario, Canada. I had radically changed my job to that of a ladies' hairstylist. One Wednesday afternoon, I worked on a client's hair for a considerable amount of time performing the tasks she had requested, and had a rather lovely discussion about people, world events and how each should be improved, when it dawned on me that this person was not arguing with me. Normally my participation created considerable—and usually hostile—rebuttals. When I enquired as to why there were no disagreements she said, "what would you say if I told you that there are thousands of people who think like you do?" My reply was, "there cannot be or I would have met them before now." She said, "you just did." To say I was flabbergasted is mild. This lady was Helen Kelly, who with her husband Dan, ran a local pharmacy. Helen explained that the people she was talking about were Bahá'ís. That triggered a memory of an article from two weeks before in the Hamilton Spectator, a local daily newspaper, about a Bahá'í wedding which described that, although there was no clergy, the Bahá'ís had received by the provincial law the right to conduct and sanctify weddings. This was interesting to me because it seemed so radical. My contact with the Kelly's continued for a further two years or so during which time I crashed a Feast and met what became many new friends, and was provided with various pieces of literature and a book called, *Bahá'u'lláh and the New Era*, which I devoured. As I read, my excitement grew and then suddenly my contact was gone. The Kelly's pioneered to Yellowknife, Northwest Territories, Canada.

My interest in the Bahá'í Faith stayed on but, because of lack of physical contact, began to wane somewhat.

Approximately two years later, on a very hot Saturday afternoon, I was working on a part-time job selling vacuum cleaners door-to-door. Since it was summer and hot, most people were out so I gave up door knocking and returned to the office where I was asked to go to a house and repair a vacuum hose. A simple job, so I went. As I was doing the repair, I noticed a beautifully framed photograph on a small corner table. This photo seemed so out of place in this house, which was very Canadian in decor. The photo was of a middle eastern man who was wearing a beard. The lady of the house kindly made some tea and we chatted about different things as I worked. After a while, a man arrived whom I recognized but it took a few minutes for me to recall where I had seen him before. Then it all came together: we had met at my first introduction to the Bahá'í community at the Feast I crashed at the Kelly's home. It was then that I remembered the picture was of 'Abdu'l-Bahá. My words of recognition exploded out of my mouth as I rushed to explain to my hosts, George and Hazel Cuttriss, who I was and how I knew them. George placed me on his monthly newsletter mailing list. I was able to stay informed as to when any firesides were being held.

I also learned that two Bahá'í families lived close to a house we rented on Fench Ave., Hamilton. They are Esme and Sid Tukeman and Dr. and Aqdas Javid.

The Javid's, new immigrants to Canada, were holding children's classes in their apartment, where I decided to take my daughters, Carol and Lesley, ages 9 and 5, respectively. The class was held every Sunday. While the classes were going on, the adults joined a fireside and had refreshments. I often joked about where I learned about the Faith: in Aqdas's bedroom.

I developed a friendship with Sid and occasionally I met him for coffee in Dundas, a town next to Hamilton. I asked a lot of questions.

In the spring of 1969, I had an intimation. It was time to "put my money where my mouth is." I called Sid and asked what I had to do to become a Bahá'í. He invited me to his house, where I signed a declaration card.

**Bob Russell**, Bradford, Ontario, Canada

# The Architect

During the war years, between 1914 and 1918, 'Abdu'l-Bahá agonized over the human slaughter and a world not heeding His advice. During these darkened days, He was moved to write a collection of teaching instructions known as *Tablets of the Divine Plan*. He wrote fourteen such Tables, eight of them in 1916, and six in 1917.

Although primarily addressed to the Bahá'ís of the United States and Canada, the scope of these Tablets extends to the world. He mentioned 120 territories and islands to be reached with the Bahá'í Message, at a time when there were Bahá'ís in only 35 countries.

The main theme of these inspiring words is that

```
The earth will become illumined with the light of
God.
```

This world-mission is no doubt a mighty task to last the whole Dispensation of Bahá'u'lláh.

The highlights of the Divine Plan are:

* Raise an army of God, equipped with the love of God, to conquer the world spiritually.
* Mentions 120 territories and islands where the Message needed to be spread.

- Identifies three conditions for success in this global campaign:

  - Firmness in the Covenant of God
  - Fellowship and love among Bahá'ís
  - Teachers must continually travel to all parts of the world

- Promises continual help from Bahá'u'lláh, the Concourse on High, and 'Abdu'l-Bahá for those who rise to this challenge.

# Don't Blame the Teacher

All Bahá'ís sincerely believe we have a spiritual message that can make the world a better place to live in. Given the problems and challenges facing all nations, it is a reasonable expectation that people from anywhere would be hungry for it. We expect the glad tidings of Bahá'u'lláh would be soaked up like water by a parched land. But this is not always the case; people are not even willing to taste, let alone digest the Bahá'í perspective. Being human, we often feel disappointed when our efforts *seem* to have no effect on others.

Often we ask, "Why does it happen?" Well, this happened to 'Abdu'l-Bahá many times. It is like a glass; when it is full, there is no room to add to it. To explain this phenomena, let's look at a story told by Stanwood Cobb, who introduced his boss to the Master.

> I was deeply interested and concerned to see what impression 'Abdu'l-Bahá would make on the owner of the school. Porter Sargent, ten years my senior, was a confirmed and positive atheist. He had been a biologist, and was suffering from that spiritual myopia which so often afflicts this type of scientist. But he was an idealist, a humanitarian, a man of great vision for humanity, and somewhat of a genius.
>
> In one intimate discussion with me on the nature of existence, during a long hike we took together on the sunny island of Capri, he had outlined to me

his concept of life and the universe.

"What do you think of it?" he asked me, with some eagerness. Perhaps this was the first occasion on which he had so fully expounded his philosophy of life.
"It is splendid!" I said. "But it only covers half of existence."
"What is the other half?"
"Spirit."
But this other half did not exist for Porter Sargent. Idealist that he was, creative-minded, somewhat of a poet—I felt sad that not one ray of spirit could penetrate the pride of his intellect.

So when this golden opportunity came of an interview with 'Abdu'l-Bahá, I had great hopes. Now, in this intimate meeting with the Master, I thought, Sargent will be forced to realize the existence of spirit. 'Abdu'l-Bahá's spiritual potency will at last penetrate his shell of scepticism.

And so, when we came out from the hotel after a half-hour conference with 'Abdu'l-Bahá, I eagerly asked, "Well, what do you think of Him?"
I have never forgotten my shattering disappointment at the answer: "He's a dear, kind, tired old man."

I was chagrined. But this experience taught me two spiritual lessons. The first was that scepticism must solve its own problems, in its own way. The second truth, even more important, was that Spirit never forces itself upon the individual. It must be invited.
   (**Cobb, Stanwood**, *Memories of 'Abdu'l-Bahá*, p. 54)

# He Listens

Earlier we saw that Bahá'u'lláh mentioned 'Abdu'l-Bahá's patience in listening to others. Let's look at an example in the words of Howard Colby Ives:

To the questioner He responded first with silence—an outward silence. His encouragement always was that the other should speak and He listens. There was never eager tenseness, the restlessness so often met showing most plainly that the listener has the pat answer ready the moment he should have a chance to utter it.

(**Blomfield**, *The Chosen Highway*, p. 136)

The attention He paid to His listener is fascinating considering His station as a human being. Here is another anecdote showing the Master's absolute patience, as told this time by Stanwood Cobb:

When 'Abdu'l-Bahá was in Boston, I seized this opportunity to take my father in to see Him, from our home in the suburb of Newton. Father at that time was a venerable Boston artist seventy-five years of age—an earnestly religious man, devout, spiritual, and prayerful. He was sympathetic to my adherence to the Bahá'í Cause, but he had said, "Son, I am too old to change." While I was in Constantinople, Father had at my request attended some of the Bahá'í meetings in Boston; and now he was glad to have this opportunity to visit with 'Abdu'l-Bahá.

But what was my consternation to perceive that Father was taking the conversation into his own hands! It was an occurrence which I never shall forget. Father for some half-hour proceeded to lay down the law to 'Abdu'l-Bahá, or let us say, to enlighten Him on spiritual themes. Or to be more exact, let us say that Father took this opportunity to express to the loving, listening ear of 'Abdu'l-Bahá the spiritual philosophy which had guided him in life. I sat there quite shocked. But I didn't need to be. 'Abdu'l-Bahá plainly was not shocked at this reversal of the customary role—He now to be the listener and His visitor the discourser. He sat there smiling, saying little, enveloping us with His love. And at the end, Father came away feeling that he had a wonderful interview. What a lesson in humility this was, that 'Abdu'l-Bahá thus exemplified! There are so many times when we can help others best just by being good listeners.

(**Cobb, Stanwood**, *Memories of 'Abdu'l-Bahá*, pp. 48-49)

# Teaching with Deeds

When studying 'Abdu'l-Bahá's life, one notices a beauty and harmony. His words were always consistent with His actions. He knew that a simple act of charity rather than hours of discourse can cause one to leap forward in the path of God.

The *Christian Commonwealth*, a London newspaper, had a special interest in the Master's travels in the west. In 1914, it carried words of praise for 'Abdu'l-Bahá.

> It is wonderful to see the venerable figure of the revered Bahá'í leader passing through the narrow streets of this ancient town ['Akká], where he lived for forty years as a political prisoner, and to note the deep respect with which he is saluted by the Turkish officials and the officers of garrison from the Governor downward, who visit him constantly and listen with the deepest attention to his words. "The Master" does not teach in Syria as he did in the West, but he goes about doing good, and Muhammadans and Christians alike share his benefactions. From sunrise often till midnight he works, in spite of broken health, never sparing himself if there is a wrong to be righted or a suffering to be relieved. To Christians who regard 'Abdu'l-Bahá with impartial and sympathetic eyes, this wonderful selfless life cannot fail to recall that life whose tragic termination on Calvary the whole Christian world recalls today.
> (*Star of the West*, Vol. III (1913-1914), p. 40)

# The First Public Speech

'Abdu'l-Bahá was a great orator, very comfortable addressing an audience. As much as speaking to individuals, He enjoyed talking to a large group. Interesting enough, His very first public speech was given on a Sunday, September 10th, 1911, from the pulpit of the City Temple in Holborn, a suburb of London. He was 67 years old. Before this time, He lived entirely in Asia, a prisoner for most of His life. He taught individuals or very small groups in His household. In the West, He found a new freedom: to talk openly about a message He loved so much.

This public appearance was both historical and unique. For the first time, the authorized leader of a world Faith had come from the East to speak to a group of people in the western world. These are His words:

O Noble friends; seekers after God! Praise be to God! Today the light of Truth is shining upon the world in its abundance; the breezes of the heavenly garden are blowing throughout all regions; the call of the Kingdom is heard in all lands, and the breath of the Holy Spirit is felt in all hearts that are faithful. The Spirit of God is giving eternal life. In this wonderful age the East is enlightened, the West is fragrant, and everywhere the soul inhales the holy perfume. The sea of the unity of mankind is lifting up its waves with joy, for there is real communication between the hearts and minds of men. The banner of the Holy Spirit is uplifted, and men see it, and are assured with the knowledge that this is a new day.

This is a new cycle of human power. All the horizons of the world are luminous, and the world will become indeed as a garden and a paradise. It is the hour of unity of the sons of men and of the drawing together of all races and all classes. You are loosed from ancient superstitions which have kept men ignorant, destroying the foundations of true humanity.

The gift of God to this enlightened age is the knowledge of the oneness of mankind and of the fundamental oneness of religion. War shall cease between nations, and by the will of God the Most Great Peace shall come; the world will be seen as a new world, and all men will live as brothers.

In the days of old an instinct for warfare was developed in the struggle with wild animals; this is no longer necessary; nay, rather, co-operation and mutual understanding are seen to produce the greatest welfare of mankind. Enmity is now the result of prejudice only.

In the *Hidden Words* Bahá'u'lláh says, 'Justice is to be loved above all.' Praise be to God, in this country the standard of justice has been raised; a great effort is being made to give all souls an equal and a true place. This is the desire of all noble natures; this is today the teaching for the East and for the West; therefore the East and the West will understand each other and reverence each other, and embrace like long-parted lovers who have found each other.

There is one God; mankind is one; the foundations of religion are one. Let us worship Him, and give praise for all His great Prophets and Messengers who have manifested His brightness and glory.

The blessing of the Eternal One be with you in all its richness, that each soul according to his measure may take freely of Him. Amen.
   (**Balyuzi, H. M.**, *'Abdu'l-Bahá*, p. 141)

This talk is a good-news message, which touches upon some of the fundamental principles such as the oneness of God, oneness of religion, oneness of mankind, abolition of wars, justice, and equality. But the most important aspect of this speech is the bright future of humanity. In fact, it is a model that can be used to prepare our own speeches.

# Word Check

| luminous | emitting light, glowing in the dark. |
|---|---|
| **superstition** | a belief that is held by a number of people but without foundation. |
| **prejudice** | an unreasoning opinion or like or dislike of something; *racial prejudice*, prejudice against people of other races. |
| **reverence** | a feeling of awe and respect or veneration. |

# Humility

'Abdu'l-Bahá, in addition to being the perfect Bahá'í Exemplar, was the Center of the Covenant and the Interpreter of the Holy Word. According to Shoghi Effendi, He had many other titles, for example, He is the "Mystery of God," "Limb of the Law of God," "round Whom all names revolve," "the Most Mighty Branch," "the incarnation of every Bahá'í virtue," and "the Ensign of the Most Great Peace."

As humans, any kind of accomplishment—spiritual, material, or intellectual—makes us feel proud of our work. Unlike us, 'Abdu'l-Bahá was able to show great humility in spite of the unique position He held in the history of mankind. He was the same to all, whether one was rich, poor, needy, or learned. Everyone got the same careful attention, full of spiritual nourishment. He exemplified humility all His life and after the passing of His Father, He preferred to be called 'Abdu'l-Bahá, the Servant of Bahá; however, His Father had asked others to call Him the Master.

# WORD CHECK

| | |
|---|---|
| **mystery** | A religious truth that is beyond human powers to understand |
| **ensign** | A special or naval flag, a special form of the national flag flown by ships. |

Humility was so much a part of His being.  He really enjoyed serving others, especially His guests, regardless of their age or position. There are countless anecdotes of His humble gestures, but we will relate only two of them here. He showed great respect and lowliness towards His Father.

At one time, Bahá'u'lláh lived in the mansion of Bahji and 'Abdu'l-Bahá in a nearby town called 'Akká. Once a week the Master would visit His Father on foot and when asked why, He said: "...who am I that I should ride where the Lord Christ walked?"

But, Bahá'u'lláh insisted that He ride. To comply to this request, He started riding from 'Akká but when sighting the mansion, He dismounted. One of Bahá'u'lláh's great pleasures was to watch His approach.
(*Bahá'í World*, Vol. IV, p. 340)

The second story is a very touching one:

One day 'Abdu'l-Bahá was going from 'Akká to Haifa and asked for a seat in the stage coach. The driver, surprised, said 'Your Excellency surely wishes a private carriage.' 'No,' replied the Master. While He was still in the coach in Haifa, a distressed fisherwoman came to Him; all day she had caught nothing and now must return to her hungry family. The Master gave her five francs, then turned to the driver and said: 'You now see the reason

why I would not take a private carriage. Why should I ride in luxury when so many are starving?'
    (**Honnold, A**., *Vignettes from the Life of 'Abdu'l-Bahá*, p. 14)

# Spiritual Nourishment

Once May Bolles (Maxwell) was on pilgrimage in 'Akká, Israel. She heard a very touching and enlightening story from 'Abdu'l-Bahá. It tells us the importance of spiritual nourishment—its effects last forever, unlike the food people eat that has only a short benefit. This story ties in with teaching someone the Faith. It demonstrates how the love of God sustains us far better than material food. 'Abdu'l-Bahá relates a story about Bahá'u'lláh and a hermit. He said:

> He passed through a lonely country where, at some little distance from the highway, a hermit lived alone in a cave. He was a holy man, and having heard that Our Lord, Bahá'u'lláh, would pass that way, he watched eagerly for His approach. When the Manifestation arrived at that spot the hermit knelt down and kissed the dust before His feet, and said to Him: "Oh, my Lord, I am a poor man living alone in a cave nearby; but henceforth I shall account myself the happiest of mortals if Thou wilt but come for a moment to my cave and bless it by Thy Presence." Then Bahá'u'lláh told the man that He would come, not for a moment but for three days, and He bade His followers cast their tents, and await His return. The poor man was so overcome with joy and gratitude that he was speechless, and led the way in humble silence to his lowly dwelling in a rock. There the Glorious One sat with him, talking to him and teaching him, and toward evening the man bethought himself that he had nothing to

offer his great Guest but some dry meat and some dark bread, and water from a spring nearby. Not knowing what to do he threw himself at the feet of his Lord and confessed his dilemma. Bahá'u'lláh comforted him and by a word bade him fetch the meat and bread and water; then the Lord of the universe partook of this frugal repast with joy and fragrance as though it had been a banquet, and during the three days of His visit they ate only of this food which seemed to the poor hermit the most delicious he had ever eaten. Bahá'u'lláh declared that He had never been more nobly entertained nor received greater hospitality and love. "*This*," exclaimed the Master, when He had finished the story, "*shows us how little man requires when he is nourished by the sweetest of all foods-the love of God.*"
(**Maxwell, May**, *An Early Pilgrimage*, pp. 23-25)

 # Word Check

| hermit | a person who has withdrawn from human society and lives in solitude. |
|--------|----------------------------------------------------------------------|
| frugal | scanty, costing little, *a frugal meal*. |
| repast | a meal. |

# Tolerance and Patience

In 1921, Professor Jakob Kunz and his wife, Anna, made a Bahá'í pilgrimage to the Holy Land where they enjoyed the presence of 'Abdu'l-Bahá. They wondered how to deal with people who denied religion.

The Master's answer was:

> You must be tolerant and patient, because the station of sight is a station of bounty; it is not based on capacity. They must be educated.
> (*Star of the West,* Vol. XIII, p. 143)

When we encounter someone without physical sight, automatically our sympathy and willingness to help and be patient are evoked. Unlike physical sight, lack of spiritual insight is not always obvious. It takes time and effort on the part of the teacher to assess the person's understanding. Comprehension of the truth must be taught.

'Abdu'l-Bahá was also very patient with all His loved ones. He is patiently waiting for us to take over where He left off. He said:

> Friends! The time is coming when I shall be no longer with you. I have done all that could be done. I have served the Cause of Bahá'u'lláh to the utmost of my ability. I have labored night and day, all the years of my life. O how I long to see the loved ones taking upon themselves the responsibilities of the Cause! Now is the time to proclaim the Kingdom of Bahá! Now is the hour of love and union!...
>
> Ah me, I am waiting, waiting, to hear the joyful tidings that the believers are the very embodiment

of sincerity and truthfulness, the incarnation of
love and amity, the living symbols of unity and
concord. Will they not gladden my heart? Will they
not satisfy my yearning? Will they not manifest my
wish? Will they not fulfil my heart's desire? Will
they not give ear to my call?  I am waiting, I am
patiently waiting.

(**Blomfield and Shoghi Effendi**, *The Passing of 'Abdu'l-Bahá*, pp. 30-31)

## Comfortable with Strangers

North America is very different in many ways from the Middle East, where
'Abdu'l-Bahá lived most of His life. During His travel to Western countries, He
felt very comfortable as if He were among the members of His own family. He
always saw the positive side of everyone. We picture Him through the eyes of
Stanwood Cobb:

Here was an Oriental in Oriental garb, a man who had been prisoner most of
His life, a character whose life was for the most part lived on a spiritual
plane so lofty as to be almost beyond our comprehension. How did this
Servant of God meet, fit into, and adjust to the objective, dynamic, and
materialistic life of America?

'Abdu'l-Bahá, upon landing in New York and being surrounded by alert and
inquisitive reporters, was perfectly at home. And why not? Is there any limit
to the power of spirit? Was not 'Abdu'l-Bahá's universal spirit as capable of
dealing with the fast-vibrating technological Occident as it had been in
dealing with the mystic and more spiritual Orient? We shall see, as this
narrative continues, how He was 'all things to all men'; protean in His
universality; thoroughly at home in every environment.

This majestic figure—in tarboosh, turban, and flowing robes—drew the
newspaper men into His aura and immediately won their favor.

"What do you think of America?" He was asked.

"I like it. Americans are optimistic. If you ask them how they are they say, 'All right!' If you ask them how things are going, they say, 'All right!' This cheerful attitude is good."

And so 'Abdu'l-Bahá won reporters' hearts and continued to do so throughout His stay in America. He never seemed to them, or was described by them, as a strange or exotic personality. He always received favorable and constructive notices from the press.

(**Cobb, Stanwood**, *Memories of 'Abdu'l-Bahá*, pp. 41-42)

 # Word Check

| garb | clothing, especially of a distinctive kind. |
|---|---|
| inquisitive | eagerly seeking knowledge. |
| protean | 1. taking many forms.<br>2. variable, versatile. |
| tarboosh | a cap like a fez, worn alone or as part of a turban. |
| turban | a man's headdress consisting of a scarf around a cap. |
| aura | a luminous radiation. |

# White Roses

One minister who came was not friendly. 'Abdu'l-Bahá answered all his questions with reserve and patience. The minister asked by what authority Bahá'u'lláh is placed with Abraham, Moses and Jesus--and 'Abdu'l-Bahá said:

> Today we believe Bahá'u'lláh to be an educator...If He has opened the doors of human hearts to a higher consciousness, He is a heavenly educator. If He has not accomplished this we are privileged to deny His claim...

Then 'Abdu'l-Bahá gave the minister an armful of white roses.
(**Gail, Marzieh**, *Dawn Over Mount Hira*, p. 190)

# Mother's Milk

Stanwood Cobb, an American Bahá'í, was on Pilgrimage to the Holy Land where he was treated as the honored guest by 'Abdu'l-Bahá. Mr. Cobb said:

> Every evening at dinner 'Abdu'l-Bahá, who did not eat at that time, helped to serve us. He went around from guest to guest, putting more food upon the plates. This is the height of Oriental hospitality, to serve an honored guest with one's own hand.

> When the meal was over, 'Abdu'l-Bahá would give us a brief talk on spiritual themes. I regret I have not a memory sufficient to recall all that He said. But I do recall two of these messages of spiritual wisdom.

> It is not enough to wish to do good. The wish should be followed by action. What would you think of a mother who said, 'How I love you, my baby!'—yet did not give it milk? Or of a penniless man, who said, 'I am going to found a great university!'

On another occasion, He spoke of the need for loving patience in the face of aggravating behavior on the part of others. "One might say, `Well, I will endure such-and-such a person so long as he is endurable.' But Bahá'ís must endure people even when they are unendurable."

Three extraordinary qualities which characterized all of 'Abdu'l-Bahá's utterances were to be found in these two brief conversations: His supreme logic; His delightful sense of humor; and the inspiring buoyancy with which He gave forth solemn pronouncements.

For instance, when He said, "But Bahá'ís must endure people even when they are unendurable." He did not look at us solemnly as if appointing us to an arduous and difficult task. Rather, He beamed upon us delightfully, as if to suggest what a joy to us it would be to act in this way!

I want to emphasize this important point—the joyousness with which 'Abdu'l-Bahá always depicted the spiritual life as He enjoined it upon us. And why not? Is man's spiritual life not in reality more joyous than any other kind of life that he can lead?

This philosophy of joy was the keynote of all of 'Abdu'l-Bahá's teaching. "Are you happy?" was His frequent greeting to his visitors. "Be happy!"

Those who were unhappy (and who of us are not at times!) would weep at this. And 'Abdu'l-Bahá would smile as if to say, "Yes, weep on. Beyond the tears is sunshine."

And sometimes He would wipe away with His own hands the tears from their wet cheeks, and they would leave His presence transfigured.
  (**Cobb, Stanwood**, *Memories of 'Abdu'l-Bahá*, p. 31)

# Word Check

| | |
|---|---|
| **aggravating** | making worse or more serious. |
| **endure** | tolerate. |
| **supreme** | highest in quality, most outstanding. |
| **buoyancy** | light-heartedness, cheerfulness. |
| **solemn** | dignified and impressive. |
| **pronouncements** | declarations. |
| **arduous** | needing much effort, laborious. |

# Heart White as Snow

A Western party went on pilgrimage to the Holy Land, Israel, where they enjoyed the love and warmth of 'Abdu'l-Bahá. Also included in this group was Robert Turner, Mrs. Hearst's African American butler, who later became the first Bahá'í of his race in the American continent.

One day the pilgrims gathered with the Master, and He noticed that Mr. Turner was not among them. "Where is Robert?", He enquired. When he came into the room, 'Abdu'l-Bahá stood up and greeted him with great affection. Robert was asked to sit with everyone else and He said: "Robert, your Lord loves you. God gave you a black skin, but a heart white as snow."

(**Honnold, A.**, *Vignettes from the Life of 'Abdu'l-Bahá'*, pp. 101-102)

# ☺ TEACHING MOMENT—NEVER TOO LATE

Between 1975 and 1977 we belonged to a teaching group that traveled to different towns showing the film *Green Light Expedition* by Rúhíyyih Khánum. One of these events took us to a small town called Bobcaygeon, north of Peterborough, Ontario, Canada. We did door-to-door direct teaching and one day we came across a lady, Ada Windover, who was 90 years old and lived with her son, Gerald, who was 65 years old. Gerald was immediately attracted to the Faith and had many questions right from the beginning. Ada was a staunch Christian with a very deep love for God. As I got to know her and develop a friendship, she became an inspiration for me. Being with her, I always felt that I had taken a trip to heaven, although she had not become a Bahá'í, yet.

I would drive 30 miles each week to do her hair and just to soak up the love that she easily gave. Gerald became a Bahá'í about 6 months after our first visit. He would constantly tell Ada, "Mother, can't you see that the lady is telling you that God has sent us a new Messenger?" She tested my sincerity for 3 years. Eventually, after three years, Ada declared herself and confided in me she wanted to make sure that I was not just out to collect another member. She was 93 years old when she declared her belief in Bahá'u'lláh and had to defend herself from her family, as they were not very supportive of her decision. Both have moved on to the next world.

**Maddie Wingett**, Peterborough, Ontario, Canada

# Summary

His whole life was preoccupied with educating—through love, care, and discourse—His listeners in spiritual truth. He always understood the hearer's needs and gave each according to his or her capacity to receive.

It is Shoghi Effendi who really let us see into the character of 'Abdu'l-Bahá, his Grandfather, as a great spiritual teacher.

> It was He, our beloved 'Abdu'l-Baha, our true and shining Exemplar, who with infinite tact and patience, whether in His public utterances or in private converse, adapted the presentation of the fundamentals of the Cause to the varying capacities and the spiritual receptivity of His hearers. He never hesitated, however, to tear the veil asunder and reveal to the spiritually ripened those challenging verities that set forth in its true light the relationship of this Supreme Revelation with the Dispensations of the past.

**(Shoghi Effendi**, *Guidance for Today and Tomorrow* , pp. 234-235)

# Word Check

| receptivity | willing to receive knowledge or ideas or suggestions, etc. |
|---|---|
| verities | the truths of something, *the old verities*. |

# TEACHING BREAK

# 3

## The Spiritual Journey

As a teacher, your primary duty is to convey the Bahá'í message the best you can to anyone who is interested. In Chapter One we saw the obligation and rewards of promoting the Cause of God. When you embark on this divine discovery process many questions arise. Does every person on this planet need to know about the Bahá'í Faith? What if one does not want to hear the message? What are the teacher's responsibilities? How many stages of development does a soul undergo? Why do some souls take a long time to recognize Bahá'u'lláh?

These and many more questions are answered in the following pages. Some of the topics are:

- The basics of the soul
- The teacher's role
- Recognizing a receptive soul
- Different development stages of the soul
- Power of prayer for the seeker
- Listening first
- Religious, political, and social trends
- The enrolment card

# Basics of a Soul

Your job as a Bahá'í teacher is to enlighten—as you have been by the light of Bahá'u'lláh—souls with the knowledge of God. *Does every human being need to hear about the Bahá'í Faith?* Every human has two basic elements: body and soul. This truth is accepted by all major religions. The teachings of every religion are primarily for the development of the soul (also called the spirit) as well as the development of a new civilization. It is our belief that at the conception of a human being, both an individual body and spirit come into being. When we physically die, our soul goes to another world, a plane more appropriate for the spirit.

In Chapter One, we discovered the answer to a fundamental question, *What is the purpose of life?* It is a query that has baffled many. According to Bahá'u'lláh and 'Abdu'l-Bahá, the answer is clear and simple. We repeat the reason for creation as stated in the short obligatory prayer:

> I bear witness, O my God, that Thou hast created me
> to know Thee and to worship Thee. I testify, at
> this moment, to my powerlessness and to Thy might,
> to my poverty and to Thy wealth.
>    (**Bahá'u'lláh**, *Bahá'í Prayers*, p. 4)

Although only Bahá'ís are obliged to recite this verse, this idea is relevant to all past religions. In fact, it is crucial to the birth, growth, and very existence of the soul. Many things in our life revolve around these two words: *know* and *worship*. Also, they are intertwined; the more you know God, the more you worship Him.

Knowing God has a direct relationship to spiritual growth. Unlike physical growth, spiritual development happens from birth to death and beyond. This growth simply means developing divine qualities, such as love, compassion, kindness, truthfulness, the kind of stuff God is made of. By growing these attributes, we naturally come to know God, which automatically translates into angelic actions.

The knowledge of God is given to humankind in different dosages according to the needs of the age. As we grow, so does our capacity to know more about our Creator. Essentially, the Prophets, as Divine Teachers, reveal more about God. Yes, everyone needs to be acquainted with the latest Divine Message. This is only fair.

# The Teacher's Role

These are some fundamental reasons for growing closer to God. As we will see in detail later, the individual is entirely responsible for his or her own spiritual growth. The teacher's job is to help the soul who is willing to travel the path suggested in the Bahá'í Faith. In a way it is like caring for a baby. It is the baby that finally does the eating, walking, learning, and talking; the adult is around to help the young one do all those things.

*Why do we have to take Bahá'u'lláh's message to the masses?* Let's first look at progressive revelation. Simply, it means God sends His Messengers to humanity successively. Each comes at a different time and place, according to the needs of the world. The well known Ones are Krishna, Buddha, Moses, Christ, and Muhammad. The latest Ones are The Báb and Bahá'u'lláh. The spiritual teachings of the Messengers are basically the same, but the intensity differs. In other words, as humankind grows collectively, so does its requirements and capacities. It is like schooling; as the student moves forward to higher classes, his or her capacity to learn increases.

The teachings of the past religions are good, but they were prescribed to benefit humanity for a limited time. This is a fundamental truth. Progressively through each religion, we know God a bit more. This makes sense—our knowledge of any subject, including God, increases gradually. Now, we have to learn about God in more depth than before through the Writings of Bahá'u'lláh. In the past, disciples of Christ, Buddha, Moses, and Muhammad discharged the task of giving Their messages to the world. Now, Bahá'ís, the disciples of Bahá'u'lláh, have been given the very same task. It is a privilege to tell other souls about the new knowledge of God.

We may think it is the greatest message in the world, but experience shows that not everyone we talk to thinks this way. One thing is very clear: the receptivity depends on one's readiness and capacity. For example, it is analogous to learning calculus; it happens when a student is ready. In fact, many came in direct contact with Bahá'u'lláh but not everyone recognized His station of prophethood. Similarly, more were blessed with the presence of 'Abdu'l-Bahá; again, different people were affected in different ways. Some saw His divine power and others saw Him as an ordinary man.

In your teaching experience, you will not always get the kind of response you expect or hope for. You will wonder whether it is your fault. You will question your ability to teach, your knowledge of the Faith, or your own spiritual capacity. In such situations be kind to yourself; too much self-analysis may dampen your spirit.

However, it is important to reflect on the effectiveness and results of your efforts. This reflection is healthy if it breeds more new ideas, refreshes your spirit and invokes encouragement. But even if it kills you inside, you must remember this: you don't control everything, especially the spiritual destiny of others. The teacher's primary goal is to share the message, not necessarily change the recipient's belief. You can lead a horse to water, but you can't make it drink. Bahá'u'lláh has very clearly stated the role of His teacher with these words:

> Consort with all men, O people of Bahá, in a spirit of friendliness and fellowship. If ye be aware of a certain truth, if ye possess a jewel, of which others are deprived, share it with them in a language of utmost kindliness and good-will. If it be accepted, if it fulfil its purpose, your object is attained. If any one should refuse it, leave him unto himself, and beseech God to guide him. Beware lest ye deal unkindly with him. A kindly tongue is

the lodestone of the hearts of men.
(**Bahá'u'lláh**, *Gleanings from the Writings of Bahá'u'lláh*, p. 289)

 # Word Check

| consort | to associate, to keep company. |
|---------|--------------------------------|
| fellowship | friendly association with others. |
| lodestone | 1. an iron ore having magnetic properties.<br>2. something that strongly attracts. |

 ## TEACHING MOMENT—AN URGENT QUESTION

In 1973-1974, my husband and I traveled and lived in Europe. We got jobs on the Canadian Air Force base at Baden-Sollingen, Germany. I worked in the warehouse pricing stock and Ray Wingett worked there, too, repairing stereo equipment for military personnel. Ray and his wife, Maddie, were pioneers to the nearby city of Baden-Baden, close to the base.

I had been on a spiritual search for some time, although I was not really consciously aware of it. I had taken a comparative religion course at university, and had made a good friend who espoused Rosicrucianism. One of my roommates at university was a Swedenborgian. I was quite dissatisfied with the Catholic religion, in which I had been raised, but despite this contact with religions that weren't mainstream, I still had not entertained the real possibility that I would not live up to the expectation that "Once a Catholic, always a Catholic." And when I heard the coffee room gossip that Ray belonged to a "weird religion," I sure wasn't interested in finding out about it! There was to be no "weird religion" for this Catholic girl.

However, Maddie would come into the warehouse and she would always be very warm and friendly towards me. Gradually, we got to know each other, and have coffee from time to time. We found that we had similar backgrounds from which we were trying to heal and we would talk for hours about the latest popular psychology theory about what made people tick. I remember her loaning me a book about one of the theories.

Maddie and Ray invited us to their home for an evening. I remember the warm hospitality and especially the homemade cookies--the sure way to get to my heart in those days. Almost out of politeness and not really wanting to know very much, I asked Maddie about her religion. She told me about the Báb and Bahá'u'lláh, and I remember thinking, "oh, sure," because the names were so different. She was sensitive enough not to talk too long. But she said, as we were leaving, that this was a religion for man in his maturity. That particular choice of words bothered me, because I was 26 years old and probably was supposed to be mature, and I really didn't feel mature! I really didn't feel settled in my life and was going through some major emotional tests.

Another time, we invited Maddie and Ray to our little apartment just off the air force base. I was becoming fairly nationalistic about being Canadian, and we had hitchhiked around Europe with Canadian flags on our knapsacks. We wanted to make sure no one mistook us for Americans. Interestingly, we met some really wonderful American people on our travels, who were very humble and conscious of the image of the "ugly American" in Europe. And, on more than one occasion, we had met Canadians whom we were not particularly proud to call our countrymen. On the evening the Wingetts visited us, I was spouting off about being a Canadian. When I had finished, Maddie said, "I am grateful to have been born in Canada, but I consider myself a citizen of the world." I almost gasped, because I recognized the truth in her statement--it cut through all insularities and prejudices. It really penetrated my soul. The seed had been sown.

Maddie and Ray left Germany for Canada a few months before we did, settling in Ontario, while we returned to Nova Scotia after several months of traveling. When we arrived in Halifax, a letter was waiting from Maddie, welcoming us home, always cheerful and always encouraging.

In one of her early letters, Maddie asked me to look up the Bahá'í community in Nova Scotia, because she wanted to know how many Bahá'ís were down there, saying she was too stuck in her own backyard to really know what was going on. I wanted to do it, because I really liked Maddie and she had asked me to, but somehow I couldn't. I guess I knew, deep down, that I wouldn't be able to just ask about statistics, I would have to know more.

It was several months, nine in fact, from the time I first asked Maddie about the Faith until I went to my first fireside. I had run into a Bahá'í at a women's conference, and had also seen a Bahá'í ad in the newspaper. I wasn't working much just then, and having a lot of time on my hands to think, my search began to re-surface. I had gone back to church, though I found it difficult to get involved. One day, I was sitting at Mass listening to the sermon, and the priest, who only knew me by sight, stared right at me, and said in very strong, fire and brimstone tones, that we need to *REALLY* pray and then REALLY listen to what God is telling us. It bothered me that he was staring at me, but I ended up taking his advice. Within a short time, I had decided to go to a Bahá'í meeting.

At the first fireside I attended in Halifax, I asked many questions, especially about how Bahá'ís regard Jesus Christ. The questions were answered fully to my satisfaction and my most urgent question: "what are we supposed to be doing with our lives?" was answered in a way which was like a mystical confirmation for me. I had a dream/vision while in Germany which involved light and feeling that I was part of the light. At the fireside, one of the young Bahá'ís answered my question by saying: "we should become channels for the light." I later learned that Bahá'í means follower of Bahá'u'lláh, and follower of the light. It was my moment of confirmation. I left the fireside feeling that I probably already was a Bahá'í. I had been loaned the book, "Bahá'u'lláh and the New Era" and by the time I had read through it a few days later, I knew for sure that this was what I had been seeking. I was ecstatic to learn that God had not left mankind alone and that He had sent a new Messenger with teachings for this day. Being from a journalist background, I was very attracted by teachings that met the needs of the times.

Within a week, I had declared my faith and was enabled to get involved very quickly by the Bahá'í community of Halifax. I phoned Maddie when I declared and she burst out in tears. But my story about Maddie doesn't end here, it only begins. We have never lived in the same community, but Maddie has really been there for me through many personal struggles in my life as a Bahá'í. I have been a Bahá'í over 22 years now, and she has never quit being in touch, mostly by letter, over the years. The letters would come several times a year and were long and expressive. She would respond to my questions, and my struggles, with sympathy and encouragement, and would relate them to her personal experiences, and especially to the Faith and the Writings. Because of our similar backgrounds, coming from unhealthy families, she could always relate to my tests. I can truly say she was one of the biggest factors in my becoming deepened as a Bahá'í and being able to stay steadfast in the Faith, in spite of my grave feelings of inadequacy and unworthiness. We have had a few visits over the years, which usually turn out to be marathons of talking and sharing. Maddie's great love and understanding have enriched my life so much, and I am so very honored and grateful that Bahá'u'lláh gave me this wonderful person as a "spiritual mother."

**Pat Verge**, Cochrane, Alberta, Canada

# Who is Ready?

We think we have the key to life's greatest mystery: the purpose of life. Because of our belief in Bahá'u'lláh, we are very confident about ourselves; we have hope for this life and we know how to prepare for the next world. These are the jewels of life that we possess. One would think that these messages would be accepted like precious gifts.

The reality is that not everyone is willing to live by this message the way we are. But it is not a hopeless situation. There are many who are willing, like yourself and other Bahá'ís around the world. From the stories in this book, we gather that many are searching for something meaningful in life—they may not know it by name. A good percentage of the population is always ready to be enlisted under the banner of Bahá'u'lláh. It is like harvesting a crop. All we have to do is find those receptive, waiting souls.

To find these seekers, you have to establish contact, for example, by striking up a conversation and asking if one has heard about the Faith. Next, ask probing questions to understand the current interest and situation of this person. Next, connect the thoughts of the person to the teachings of the Faith. Always remember that what you consider important may not necessarily be relevant or interesting. For example, while unity of mankind may be your favorite subject, it may not be interesting to someone else. Each one is at a different stage of development and may not perceive reality the same way you do.

If you see some interest, you may want to proceed with more discussion, offer literature, or introduce this soul to the Bahá'í community. If there is no interest, leave it on a positive note.

# Don't be Pushy

The Faith gives us a clear purpose in life, with enough hope for this world and hereafter. We enjoy a very healthy community environment, a comfortable place to grow spiritually with a world vision. It also gives us guidance in all kinds of human behaviors. Given all these benefits, it is difficult not to be enthusiastic about our religion and offer this buffet of goodness to others.

Perhaps the most heart-rending experience is when our loved ones—spouse, friends, parents, and children—cannot see the benefits the way we see them. Sometimes we may be a bit persistent with them, although these souls may not be ready. There is a great risk in being too pushy, although your intentions may be good. If someone does not recognize the Faith for what it is, in most cases the reason is simple: their spiritual sight is not developed enough to see it. As we have discussed earlier, the best solution is to be patient and pray for the spiritual development of the person.

You may think you know the other person enough so that he or she should accept it. It is important to be sensitive to the capacity of others and give the message, in the right dosage. Otherwise, you risk alienating someone from the Faith who otherwise may find some comfort in it. The damage may last a long time and the teacher lives to regret it. It is equally paramount to recognize the difference between a polite response to your offer and a genuine interest in knowing more about the Faith. Here is a piece of advice from Bahá'u'lláh:

> Every person who in some degree turneth towards the truth can himself later comprehend most of what he seeketh. However, if at the outset a word is uttered beyond his capacity, he will refuse to hear it and will arise in opposition.
> (**Bahá'u'lláh**, *The Individual and Teaching*, p. 3)

# An Independent Journey

The spiritual journey that we are all engaged in is really about a personal relationship between a soul and its Creator. Bahá'u'lláh attests to this in the following passages:

> O SON OF MAN!
> I loved thy creation, hence I created thee. Wherefore, do thou love Me, that I may name thy

name and fill thy soul with the spirit of life.
  (**Bahá'u'lláh**, *Hidden Words*, Arabic # 4)

O SON OF BEING!
Love Me, that I may love thee. If thou lovest Me
not, My love can in no wise reach thee. Know this,
O servant.
  (**Bahá'u'lláh**, *Hidden Words*, Arabic # 5)

O SON OF BEING!
Thy Paradise is My love; thy heavenly home, reunion
with Me. Enter therein and tarry not. This is that
which hath been destined for thee in Our kingdom
above and Our exalted dominion.
  (**Bahá'u'lláh**, *Hidden Words*, Arabic # 6)

O SON OF SPIRIT!
My claim on thee is great, it cannot be forgotten.
My grace to thee is plenteous, it cannot be veiled.
My love has made in thee its home, it cannot be
concealed. My light is manifest to thee, it cannot
be obscured.
  (**Bahá'u'lláh**, *Hidden Words*, Arabic # 20)

Thus doth the Nightingale utter His call unto you
from this prison. He hath but to deliver this clear
message. Whosoever desireth, let him turn aside
from this counsel and whosoever desireth let him
choose the path to his Lord.
  (**Bahá'u'lláh**, *Bahá'í Prayers: Tablet of Ahmad,* p. 209)

One thing is very clear from these Words. Each soul's approach towards God is
totally independent of others; one can choose to turn towards or away from the
path of God. This truth applies not just to Bahá'í's but every soul on this planet.

The relationship between God and His creatures is close and personal, and there is no room for a third party.

In fact, independent investigation of the truth is a cardinal principle of the Bahá'í Faith. And we have to respect this God-given right. Therefore, the teacher's responsibility is only to help a soul in this process, not for how this help is received. However, we need to choose our words with utmost care. Bahá'u'lláh said:

> One word is like unto springtime causing the tender saplings of the rose-garden of knowledge to become verdant and flourishing, while another word is even as a deadly poison.
>
> (**Bahá'u'lláh**, *Gleanings from the Writings of Bahá'u'lláh*, pp. 172-173)

# Different Development Stages of a Soul

We are as unique as the leaves on a tree or the grains of sand on a beach. So is the spiritual quest of each of us unique. In 1906, Stanwood Cobb, while studying for the Unitarian ministry at Harvard Divinity School, accepted the Bahá'í Faith by hearing these words: "The Lord has come." Some have accepted it through dreams, yet others have taken decades to make the final step of acceptance. No situation is better than the other; the most important move is that one acknowledges the Messenger of God for this day.

The teaching job is not over after someone hears about the Faith, but it continues until their belief is firmly established in Bahá'u'lláh as the Manifestation of God. The stages a soul travels can  be loosely defined into four categories: search, acceptance, nurturing, and confirmation. In the following sections we will see how you, as a teacher, can participate in each of these phases.

# *Search*

Search means looking for something better in life. We all go through it at one time or another in our lives and sometimes many times. It is a healthy process of growth. It is a sign of development; without it a human being becomes stagnant.

*What do we search for?* Many have different quests at different stages of their lives, but the essence of this process remains the same: one is not satisfied with the current situation. One yearns for some improvements to one's life, such as pursuit of happiness, better education, more independence, spirituality. These yearnings can also be external, such as the desire to bring changes to society. One may not be happy with politics, the lack of harmony among races, or with rituals of religions, for example.

Finding ways of improving one's life and society is very healthy—the key to the progress of humankind. However, too much questioning without any action is neurotic and may lead individuals or society to self-abuse.

*How to satisfy the search?* The path to enlightenment depends on the individual. There are many paths: making more money, joining politics, finding a better job, and so on. Some do investigate religion as a way to quench the thirst of search.

The moment of search is the time when we sow the seed of the Faith in the seeker's mind. Some do give the Bahá'í Faith, with its modern and logical approach to human concerns, a chance, and even join if it suits the individual's needs at that particular time.

# *Acceptance*

Joining the Bahá'í Faith is an easy step. There are two requirements: acceptance of Bahá'u'lláh as the latest Manifestation from God and awareness of the laws, principles and teachings of His Revelation. Shoghi Effendi has clearly explained the process of acceptance:

> He feels that those responsible for accepting new
> believers should consider that the most important
> and fundamental qualification for acceptance is
> the recognition of the station of Bahá'u'lláh...
> The early believers in both the east and
> west...knew practically nothing...yet they were
> the ones who shed their blood...Therefore, those
> responsible for accepting new enrolments must be
> sure of just one thing—that the heart of the
> applicant has been touched with the spirit of the
> Faith. Everything else can be built on this
> foundation gradually.
>
> (**Shoghi Effendi**, *A Special Measure of Love*, p. 20)

 # Word Check

| fundamental | 1. of the basis or foundation of a subject, etc., serving as a starting point.<br>2. very important, essential. |
| --- | --- |

The acceptance can happen anywhere—on a bus, under a tree, street, or home. There is no prescribed place or ritual to follow. At times, it sounds like a formality, but its importance in one's life cannot be underestimated. It is a spiritual rebirth. If one wants to celebrate this occasion, it is perfectly acceptable.

After declaring one's faith in Bahá'u'lláh and enrolling as a member of the community, the soul faces a new set of challenges, adapting to the teachings of a new religion and the environment of a different community. This stage is crucial, and the teacher's job is not done yet.

Some of these challenges are:

- Accepting a new belief system.
- Associating with a new group of people.
- Replacing some old habits and behaviors with new ones that are more in line with the Bahá'í Faith.
- Getting rid of prejudices and associating with members of different races.
- Emphasizing spirituality instead of materialism in life.

In time of spiritual crisis, one should have someone to turn to. This could be a teacher or someone else. Like a newborn, the soul needs to be nurtured, without which it won't survive the second birth. Of course, the Institutions of the Faith, like the Local Assembly and Auxiliary Board member or assistant to an Auxiliary Board member, must always be watching new declarants with keen eyes. If they see any signs of difficulty, they should help. One of those signs is when new believers stop participating in Bahá'í events. They may also express their difficulties in conversation in subtle ways and we need to be sensitive and aware so that we can pick up on these clues.

## Nurturing

Nurturing a soul is not easy. Unlike nurturing a baby, you are dealing with adults and youth, and there are no clear-cut steps. In this area we have a lot to learn. We cannot underestimate this stage. If the Bahá'í community is not able to handle this effectively, many will enter the Faith and some will become inactive. Although statistical numbers may look good, the net result will be a growing community with many unconfirmed believers. Here are some difficulties the new believer may experience:

- Prayer.
- Difficulty reconciling the differences between the old and the new.
- Difficulty assimilating into the new community because the cultural

differences may be overwhelming.
- Inability to get rid of old habits like consuming alcohol or drugs.
- Lack of understanding of certain Bahá'í principles.

Some ideas for nurturing are:

- Love, comfort and fellowship.
- Turn to the Writings for answers.
- Bahá'ís are not perfect beings. Everyone—old and new—is trying to apply the teachings the best way they can. Sometimes we fail and other times we succeed. No Bahá'í community is perfect and it will require a lot of work to make it a heaven on earth.
- Encourage participation in summer schools, conferences, visiting other communities, to broaden one's outlook.
- Remind new believer that his or her faith must be firmly based on belief in Bahá'u'lláh while developing his or her relationship with Him, and not on the personalities of individual Bahá'ís or communities.

## Confirmation

At this stage in one's spiritual development, one has reached the point of no return. It is a point when one has no doubt about the station of Bahá'u'lláh. It is as clear to the believer as the light of the sun that Bahá'u'lláh is the Prophet for this day. Even were the whole world to deny it, she would still continue to believe. Even if the whole world turned against her, she would still continue to consider Bahá'u'lláh as the return of all the past Prophets. She would very gladly give her life instead of recanting her belief.

At this stage, it does not mean one is a perfect Bahá'í, rather one reaches an unwavering conviction about the station of Bahá'u'lláh and a loyalty to the Covenant of God. She will try to abide by all the laws and live according to His teachings.

If she finds other Bahá'ís become a test, she will not withdraw from the community. Rather, she sees this as an opportunity to improve her Bahá'í community life. This way she is not only growing spiritually, but also helping the life of humankind. This is the ultimate stage to reach on this earthly plane.

## Prayer for the Soul

Prayers are essential in the spiritual development of any soul. They draw upon the help of the Holy Spirit in finding the receptive souls. You can offer prayers for those you are teaching, to assist their quest for truth. Acknowledging the truth is not always an easy task. Some of us have to go through much internal contemplation—and perhaps turmoil—before reaching a conclusion.

# TEACHING MOMENT—LITERALLY

# PRAYED INTO THE FAITH

My parents, Milner and Helen Barker, became Bahá'ís on May 2, 1978, the 12th day of Ridván. They were literally prayed into the Faith.

They befriended a Persian family from another area. For about one year and a half they attended every Bahá'í activity, from Toronto to Barrie in Ontario, Canada. The man prayed every day for my parents to become Bahá'ís. He wanted them to join before the end of Ridván of that year.

Well, April 21 (1st day of Ridván) came and went without anything happening. Then the 9th day passed by. Then the 12th day came and I was getting skeptical about the plan.

On the last day of Ridván, after supper at my parents', I looked outside and the sun was beginning to set. They suggested we play a game of scrabble. When I took the board, I saw inside two declaration cards.

Immediately I ran to the window. The sun was just hanging in the sky above the horizon ready to disappear into the night. I dashed to the phone, yelling to my parents that I had to make a long distance call to the Persian man. My parents were rather perplexed, given the momentous occasion.

I connected with the man, who was called out of a Local Spiritual Assembly meeting. I had to tell him that my parents became Bahá'ís before the end of Ridván and he had literally prayed them into the Faith.

**Carol Barker**, Gloucester, Ontario, Canada

# Listen, Listen, Listen

In this modern age we lead a very busy life. We often hear people say, "So many things to do and not enough time to do them all." Time has become very precious. People may *only* allow time for your message if they feel you can benefit them in any way.

Before offering anything, first find out what the immediate needs of the listener are and then see how the Faith can help. If you show how their concerns—short or long term—can be addressed through the teachings of the Bahá'í Faith, you will definitely have an attentive listener. For example, if you offer to share a few Bahá'í prayers for children with a mother with a newborn, you will grab her attention more than explaining that world unity and peace is possible. Let's look at another example. If you come across someone grieving over a lost loved one, perhaps that person would be more interested in the Bahá'í perspective of life-after-death rather than on a universal judicial system.

The main point is that your success in teaching will increase when you say the right thing at the right time. Sometimes it is very tempting to give someone all the gems you have discovered and consider to be very important. But if your audience is not at all interested, it will only amount to dumping your knowledge on someone's ear. Fortunately, the Bahá'í Faith has explanations on a wide variety of subjects, some very specific and others broad spiritual guidance.

In the previous chapter we saw how 'Abdu'l-Bahá was a great listener, a quality greatly admired by Bahá'u'lláh. He gave the right prescription for each situation. It is a skill not easily acquired, but very useful. In Chapter One, we also saw how the Holy Spirit is always ready to inspire us to say the right thing. This is a promise of Bahá'u'lláh available to any teacher at any time. A teacher can take advantage of this divine help.

# Religious, Political, Social, and Technological Trends

Earlier, we discussed the internal needs of a searching soul. A teacher must also be aware of the external environment. Internal beliefs and social trends exert influence on each other. One thing is certain about the world: it is changing fast. This century is very different from the past; life has been completely revolutionized in the last hundred years. The alterations are so pervasive that there are very few things we do now that are the same as a hundred years ago, a reference point for our discussion here. Let's look at a few examples. We eat as always, but in most places the diet is different. Now we have McDonalds, Kentucky Fried Chicken, Chinese food, pizza, and Mexican food becoming popular around the world. Even our local dishes are being changed by outside influences. Then, we traveled by trains, ships, animals, and bicycles. Now, we do all those things and also have fast cars, planes, and trains. We communicated with letters, messengers, and telegraph. Nowadays, telephone, Internet, fax, satellite, cellular phone, television, electronic mail, and radio are some of the ways people interact with each after at lighting speed.

The transformation of the 20th century is so extensive and profound that countless volumes have already been written and more will be written as we unravel the implications of these world-shaking changes. This century has witnessed the most triumphant and trying moments of human life. They can only be described by superlative words.

We witnessed the greatest devastation of the two world wars. From the ashes of battle fields came the United Nations, a new global concept of government. In the last hundred years, many kings and dictators have been replaced by democratic governments. The same century has witnessed the rise and the fall of the Soviet Union, a very powerful communist block, the collapse of apartheid in South Africa, and crumbling of the Berlin Wall, which separated East and West Germany.

Many citizens of good will around the world have sacrificed blood, tears, and labor to promote human rights on this planet and to ensure the dignity that every human being deserves, regardless of one's background, color, and creed. This has given rise to organizations such as Amnesty International. Many governments have included human rights as a fundamental part of their constitutions. We have also seen women—one half of world's population—fighting for equality. They have shown, in spite of opposition, that they can be world leaders in politics, science, and education, positions until now mostly held by men.

We witnessed the sun set on the British Empire, the largest empire to rule the world. This gave rise to many independent countries, some big, like India and China, others small like Mauritius, Malta, and Seychelles. Subsequently, other European Empires had to relinquish their dominions. Breaking up of empires gave way to new-born countries spread all over Africa, Asia, North and South America, and many oceans. More people were given a chance to govern their own destiny rather than being ruled by foreigners.

Education flourished. More gained access to primary, secondary, and university education. Successively, more people were educated than the previous generation.

Warring religious groups have found ways to come together in dialogue. Jews and

Christians are sitting together to discuss common points of concern. Protestants and Catholics have attempted to settle their differences. Some of these events were inconceivable at the turn of this century. In the West, more people are familiar with Eastern religions, like Hinduism, Buddhism, and Islam. Scientists and religious leaders are getting together to discuss common issues that lead to better understanding of reality, both metaphysical and physical.

Humans have landed on the moon, something that seemed impossible because of lack of technology before the `40's and `50's. Now, space travel is a routine event. Satellites hover hundred of miles above earth forming a network of communication devices that help us with our telephone conversations, TV programs, and data transfers around the world. These would have been unimaginable just a hundred years ago.

Medicine has made major advances, making transplants of human organs common. Many life threatening diseases like tuberculosis, polio, and malaria have been eradicated in most parts of the world. We have sophisticated machines like the CAT SCAN to detect cancer. There are drugs to cure many of the ills of our time. Both medical professionals and common folks are more aware of the importance of good health.

Telecommunication and computers, two of the fastest growing technologies, are the key components of the much-talked-about Information Highway. The new form of electronic communication is further shrinking the world through Internet and WEB sites, making transfer of information instantaneous across the world. This is a totally new experience for humans; we have seen nothing like this. What are the implications? This technology has become a powerful tool to share experience and knowledge to solve worldwide economic, social and political problems.

In recent years, Internet, WEB sites, and the Information Highway have become household words—but they have existed for decades—tying many academic research centers together.

Another major development is world trade and the world economy. For many decades Western Europe and North America had been economic powers of enormous proportions. They had been ruling the world. In the last few decades, we have seen a major shift: many emerging countries are fast becoming world economic forces. Some of them are China, India, Singapore, Japan, Hong Kong, and Korea. Because of liberalized free trade, we see free movement of capital and goods around the world. Let's look at auto manufacturing. World class companies like Toyota, General Motors, Volvo, and Volkswagen have plants, not only in their native countries, but also around the world. Global trade is a very lucrative business for multinational companies.

To facilitate trade there are many international agreements among countries in Europe, North and South America, and Asia. In fact, it is a growing trend to involve all countries with the General Agreements on Trade and Tariff (GATT).

To facilitate this new economy, many organizations are emerging to determine global rules and conventions. One prominent example is the World Trade Organization, which deals with labor standards and trade, the environment and trade, policies in foreign investment and multinationals, competition policies, the issue of giving trade advantages to the poorest developing countries, and the possibility of free trade in information technologies.

The events of this century are so numerous that they cannot all be listed here, let alone discussed for their implications in our daily lives. There is an explosion of information; every few years the amount of knowledge is doubling on all fronts. If we were to bring back some of our past heroes, such as Henry Ford, Alexander Graham Bell, Mahatma Gandhi, Albert Schweitzer, John Lennon, and Martin Luther King, they would be dumbfounded by one thing: this world is so different than when they left. And it is changing ever more rapidly at breakneck speed.

By no means has heaven descended on earth. There are still many problems plaguing mankind. Some have persisted for decades, with no solution in sight. Arabs and Jews are still fighting in the Middle East. Millions are still stricken with poverty in many parts of the world while there is abundance of food elsewhere. There still are inequalities. Human rights are still being violated. Ethnic wars still are destroying many societies. In many areas, including the

United States, race harmony is still very elusive. Other issues are coming to the surface that did not exist one hundred years ago. We have endless and sometimes furious discussion about environment, abortion, drug abuse, homosexual rights, euthanasia (death by choice), and so on. It seems humans are faced with whirlwinds of changes; some are beneficial while others are destructive.

*What is happening to the world?* This question bothers many of us, but few have a clear answer. Bahá'ís know exactly what is happening. The world is going through a complete transformation, propelled by the spirit of a new revelation. After the long winter of the previous dispensation, we are in the springtime of a new Faith. We are exposed to the heat and rays of a new day, bringing to life all aspects of human affairs. We are seeing the signs of many things that Bahá'u'lláh talked about over one hundred years ago:

- Spiritualization of the planet
- World government and economy
- End of all kinds of prejudices
- Equality of sexes
- Harmony among religions
- Harmony between science and religion

A new plan for this earth has been released and the final stage is no less than The Most Great Peace. According to Bahá'u'lláh, this should happen over the next thousand years. Of course, we are at a very early stage of this mighty divine plan. The task is the construction of the new infrastructures that will support the new world order. Bahá'ís are very aware of this prediction of the future, hence we understand the changes. But the rest of the world is experiencing them too, without any knowledge of this plan or the direction of future events. We are part of a mighty plan.

This divine whirlwind brings different issues to the surface at different stages. As a teacher, you have to be aware of which way the divine wind is blowing. To explain a bit further, let's look at two examples. First, when Táhirih, a Letter of Living in the Bábí Dispensation, was murdered by her attackers, she said these prophetic words, "You can kill me as soon as you like, but you cannot stop the emancipation of women!" (**Shoghi Effendi**, *God Passes By*, p. 75). Then equality of men and women was as unimaginable as landing on the moon. Now, both are possible. Although equality the way Bahá'u'lláh has envisioned has a long way to go to be realized, humans are now definitely working towards this divine goal.

Second, just a few decades ago when Bahá'ís explained why involvement in politics is not the right avenue for permanent changes, this idea did not make sense. Politics had always been considered the primary way in democratic societies to bring about reforms. Now, there is unprecedented contempt for and mistrust of politicians in many parts of the world. Some are even targets of ridicule. This Bahá'í concept of non-participation in politics not only is easier to understand now, but it makes more sense.

Other hot topics these days are education of children, life-after-death, world trade, ethnic cleansing. Someday these issues will go away and we will be in the midst of some other debates. This will go on for a long time. Being aware of the changes that are happening in our community, country and the world, helps us to connect with the concerns of those we are teaching. It will certainly give us more opportunities to promote the Cause of God.

 ## TEACHING MOMENT—GETTING PAID TO BECOME BAHÁ'Í

When my parents became old and sold their farm in 1949, I quit teaching school to go help them move to Forest, Ontario, Canada.

For many years my late mother used to be a correspondent for one of the local newspapers, The Forest Free Press. I started to operate the linotype for the newspaper, as the owners, the Pettypiece family, were friends of our family for three generations.

When I wasn't printing the local news, they had me print type on a rather strange sounding name—The Canadian Bahá'í News. And I had to read the stuff to print it. Of course I was getting paid to type this publication, and I became just a bit curious. Eventually I started to ask questions. New concepts were presented to me by fellow workers. Later I realized these fellow workers were also of the Bahá'í World Faith. They are Leslie and Ada Hinchcliffe, John and Kathy Hoyle, and Harper and Joan Pettypiece.

My father all his life had been a Scotch Presbyterian and my mother of the Methodist faith. We could not skate on Sundays; we could read our Sunday School lesson and the Bible. There was no card playing in our home. However, I have happy memories of my childhood.

Eventually I signed a Bahá'í declaration card and have been active since that date, although in my new work I keep contact and report on special events of all the churches of the area.

**Floyd MacIntyre**, Forest, Ontario, Canada

# The Enrolment Card

Sometimes teaching seems like walking on a tight rope: you don't want to be pushy at the risk of losing a chance for someone to join the Faith. Most people we teach don't know the procedure of becoming a Bahá'í. Some may think there is a special ritual; others may think they have to change their name to be a member of the Faith; or just being with Bahá'ís means to be part of the religion. Unless we clarify this point, they may have all kinds of notions and not know the simple, proper way.

To become a Bahá'í, all that is required is to acknowledge Bahá'u'lláh as the latest Manifestation of God. The place it happens is in one's heart. To inform the administration of this fact, one has to fill out a form. Once accepted by a Local Spiritual Assembly (or National Spiritual Assembly where a Local Assembly does not exist), one can fully participate in the community. At this point, the new Bahá'í can contribute to the Funds, attend Feasts, and participate in elections, privileges only held by Bahá'ís. Remember, one may profess to accept Bahá'u'lláh, but without the formal declaration, one cannot participate in these activities.

It is important to make the would-be-Bahá'í aware of the declaration card. Of course, the teacher has to do it at an appropriate time; if done in a sensitive way, no one will be offended. Here is a clear instruction on enrollment:

> The prime motive should always be the response of man to God's Message, and the recognition of His Messenger. Those who declare themselves as Bahá'ís should become enchanted with the beauty of the teachings, and touched by the love of Bahá'u'lláh. The declarants need not know all the proofs, history, laws, and principles of the Faith, but in the process of declaring themselves they must, in addition to catching the spark of faith, become basically informed about the Central Figures of the Faith, as well as the existence of laws they must follow and an administration they must obey.
>
> (**The Universal House of Justice**, *Wellspring of Guidance*, p. 32)

# Word Check

| recognition | recognizing, being recognized. |
|---|---|
| enchanted | 1. put under a magic spell. <br> 2. filled with intense delight. |

## Summary

We just discussed the turbulent times we are undergoing. A Bahá'í teacher is faced with a major problem of convincing others that the propelling force behind the changes is Bahá'u'lláh's revelation. So many positive and negative phenomena are happening in front of us and the Bahá'ís are the only ones aware of their origin. But once one becomes a Bahá'í, everything becomes clear, as if all the clouds from the sky have been lifted.

*What do we offer?* To a searching soul we offer the true spirit, the real life of a human being. On this journey towards the knowledge of God, there are many obstacles and difficulties. The teacher has to be aware of the nature of the soul and its requirements. Equally important is to know the different stages a soul progresses through before it is ready to accept the Faith. On this journey, we all need help at one time or another.

The teacher's job is to help the soul, respectful of the God-given free-will of each person and the personal nature of the relationship between each soul and its Creator.

# TEACHING BREAK

"I KNOW I PUT THAT ENROLLMENT CARD SOMEWHERE!"

# 4

# Opportunities Unlimited

One of the most challenging issues at this point of Bahá'í history is to take Bahá'u'lláh's great message to the entire world. Just the numbers tell us there is a big job ahead of us. In this planetary task, there are three mind-boggling aspects. One is that there are only a few million Bahá'ís in a world of six billion population and growing. Second, the rate of growth of the world population is faster than the Bahá'ís. Third, we don't have career teachers like other religions do. Some do take this job full-time, but only for a short time. The rest of us, including the pioneers, have to teach on a part-time basis after taking care of daily work.

One strategy is to find opportunities to meet people who are not Bahá'ís, yet, and tell them about the Good News: the Promised One of all ages has come. Where to meet people who are not Bahá'ís? Obviously, there are plenty of opportunities. Just look at the numbers. Given the urgency, it seems we must be very effective by looking for those who are ripe to be taught, and we have assurances from 'Abdu'l-Bahá that there are many such souls out there. The stories in this book also testify to this truth. In this chapter we will look at some of these ways to meet people and how to take the best advantage of them. They are:

- Workplace
- Educational institutions
- Bahá'í Holy Days and New Year
- Christmas parties, sporting and cultural events

- Friends and family members
- Ethnic and religious groups
- Organizations

# Workplace

A workplace can provide you with many opportunities to teach the Bahá'í Faith. Of course, this would apply if you are not working at Bahá'í Institutions where everyone is a Bahá'í. You see your co-workers daily and probably have established a relationship with them. With time you get to know some of them very well. On occasion, the relationship can change from just being co-workers to friends.

People do notice Bahá'ís are different from the rest. How many times have we heard from someone who knows a Bahá'í: "Bahá'ís are nice people." This is a credit to our community.

The workplace can be a harsh environment for service. Although the workplace is constantly improving through new techniques such as teamwork, empowerment of individuals, and better communications, yet it does breed competition, promote office politics, backbiting, and so on. Sometimes work pressure can be intense enough that one unwillingly has to compromise other obligations such as family life.

As Bahá'ís, our attitude towards work is different. To us, work is considered the same as worship to God when carried out as a service to society. We do our task as best we can without competing with one another or siding with anyone or any group in disputes; rather we try to deal with people with fairness and respect. We will help someone rather than harm them. We seek cooperation. In spite of the pressures of an ever-changing workplace, we try to maintain a balance between work and personal obligations. People notice our different life style which is tempered with a spirit of friendliness. They become curious because humans have the perpetual desire to improve their lives.

You may ask: "Should I promote religion at work?" You are there primarily to work. It is a question you must give some thought to if you come across someone with whom you would like to share the Bahá'í message. It would be advisable not to teach the Faith during the working hours for which you are getting paid. If you feel comfortable, you can invite your co-worker for lunch or coffee. Inviting one to your home might be an even better idea. Away from work, it gives you a chance to introduce the Bahá'í Faith in a more relaxed environment. If there is any kind of interest, you might follow it up with more discussion, giving literature and so on.

There are many ways to introduce the Faith to your co-workers, for example, mentioning our New Year, Holy Days, things that we do differently and so on.

# High School, College, and University

This is a great fertile place to teach. It is where young people are open to new ideas and approaches to life's problems. It is a place of learning—this environment provides a great opportunity to present Bahá'í ideas, which are really new perspectives on life, in many different ways.

First, you come in contact with students, staff and faculty members. Over a period of time, you establish some kind of a relationship. With your classmates, there are chances of developing strong friendships that might last a lifetime. Generally, academic populations are liberal minded and likely open to notions of a new world religion originating in the East. The university also has a very diverse population, a chance to meet students from many different parts of the world. Promoting unity of races and abolition of prejudices may be very relevant.

Secondly, join the Bahá'í club of the campus. If one does not exist, it is an excellent opportunity to form one. This gives the Faith some legitimacy and status. Colleges and universities are fertile grounds of new ideas. Perhaps it would be worth your while to explore common ground with other clubs and plan events together. This will give the Bahá'ís opportunities to expand the number of contacts who will learn about the Faith. Other ideas are:

- foster scholarship in the Bahá'í Writings.
- advance the process of entry by troops on campus.
- Regular weekly firesides.
- Ongoing series of symposiums put on every semester. You can invite other departments and clubs at school to co-sponsor the symposium. One format for such an event can be a keynote address and a panel discussion with panelists of different backgrounds. Example of topics are: "Prosperity of Humankind" and "Turning Point for All Nations." This way the Bahá'í Club can demonstrate to a large audience the relevance and depth of Bahá'í thought on different current issues. A side benefit of the symposium can be to increase your fireside attendance.
- Write articles for the school newspaper. With this vehicle you can reach a larger audience to create more awareness and interest.
- Participate in radio programs.
- Place booths and displays in strategic places.
- Give annual awards on behalf of ABS (Association for Bahá'í Studies) to individuals showing dedication to world citizenship or community service.
- have luncheons with groups of interested faculty and attempt to get Bahá'í courses or Bahá'í content into courses.

If you are not part of a campus but live close to one, you may find some good teaching opportunities. First, you can help the Bahá'í Campus Club with their activities. This will give you a good reason to be part of the campus. You can meet all kinds of people, especially foreign students, who want to taste life outside the campus. You can get to know them and perhaps invite them to firesides and meetings.

# TEACHING MOMENT—JESUS NEVER LIVED

I attended Sunday School and the United Church with my family during childhood, but around the time of political questioning I read a book from the public library: "Did Jesus Ever Live?" It made such a good case that I decided that He hadn't. I concluded that it didn't matter and that I was an agnostic. It was enough that these good teachings were in the world. It became clear that something was needed in the form of a religion that worked in our time, would do away with war and social injustice and would have the power that religions have to change the hearts of people. I knew that only something bigger than humans could make them behave. These conclusions I reached alone in my own mind and I didn't discuss them with anybody.

It seemed that I should start to examine the world religions. I set a test -- it had to make sense to my common sense, and it had to be working in the present day. Past effects and glories didn't count. As soon as I found something I just couldn't swallow I would reject the whole thing. I examined anything I heard of, so long as it met my criteria, but as soon as it didn't I would drop it immediately and keep on with my search.

I read about the various world religions and other groups. You have to remember that I was just fifteen and not a scholar, so I just studied whatever I could get my hands on and dropped one after the other as they seemed to fail my tests. I didn't even consider Christianity because I could see all around me that it hadn't passed the tests, and furthermore, I had been over-exposed to an evangelical girlfriend. These tests became like an archway through which I could walk away and on to the next and I began to expect it.

One summer evening, of the year I turned 16 I suppose, I attended a corn roast sponsored by the political party. I met Alan Griffiths who knew my parents and who had noticed me before. He invited me to a Bahá'í corn roast the next night. I thought that he said "Bi Y" and that it was some club of the YM/YWCA, or I might not have gone. Mine was a solitary search and there were two words I was very uncomfortable with saying out loud, one was God and the other was love.

He took me to a cottage on the shores of Lake Ontario at the end of Fire Lane 300. I think that is remarkable because we moved and lived within yards of the place within a year. The rented cottage was lent to the Bahá'ís by a Bahá'í friend named Marg Hardy. It turned out to be a going away party for Aldie Robarts who was leaving to join his parents in Africa. I had a wonderful time and liked the people I met who seemed to be individualists, (rare birds in my young life in the early 50's)! Finally I realized that it was a religious group called "Bahá'ís" who were holding the party, but I wouldn't ask a thing and nobody told me anything. I had somehow learned that religion was a thing you didn't discuss (but not politics!) but I really liked Alan and I was intensely curious about the Bahá'í Faith. I tried everywhere to find out about it. There was nothing to be found. On a school trip to Toronto, Ontario, I enquired in a large book store. Nothing. I bought a book about Madame Blavatsky's group, but they knew nothing in the store about the Bahá'í Faith.

Alan continued to invite me on dates and I was finally driven to asking him what the Bahá'í Faith was. From then on, we spent all of our evenings talking about it until late hours. I would think about it during the day until I was sure I had found the flaw. When I confronted him triumphantly with it in the evening he was always able to explain things so thoroughly to my satisfaction that I usually reversed sides and began telling him additional reasons for the rightness of his answers. We went on for a long time like that. I borrowed books. Finally he invited me to a public meeting in the Sheraton Brock Hotel in Niagara Falls; another Sunday it was to a hotel in Welland; again to the Kate Leonard Room in the YWCA in St. Catharines. There, I heard people like Laura Davis and Lloyd Gardner. I was more and more interested and he took me to my first fireside in St.

Catharines at Jean Smith's apartment on Geneva Street. I began to attend them every Tuesday evening. I met Charlie Grindlay at my first fireside. It was his second one. They were wonderful!

Jean, (sister to Lloyd Gardner's wife, Helen) was the lone Bahá'í in St. Catharines, a shy person of few words, and she always had some non-Bahá'í apartment sharer, yet she steadfastly held the firesides and attracted all kinds of people to them through her sports activities. She was the Canadian table tennis champion and also played badminton. She was Secretary-Treasurer of Slazengers Canada Ltd. and eventually hired me for my first full time job when I came out of school at the end of Grade eleven. Both my parents had life-threatening illnesses and so I had to take the secretarial course (although my school principal approached my father and told him that I should go to university) and then stop a year before graduation so that I could get work in case I needed to take care of my twin brothers, seven years younger than myself. That's the kind of sacrifice that girls traditionally have been called to make.

I continued every Tuesday to travel downtown from my job, eat alone in a restaurant and walk a couple of miles to Jean's firesides. They were supported by young Bahá'ís from the University of Western Ontario in London, Ontario, who often drove over and back the same night, for the evening firesides. I often met Doug Martin, Betty (Martin), Doug Wilson, Dianna Merrick (Dainty), Marjory Merrick, her mother, Don Dainty, Margie Parkhill (East), Elizabeth Manser (Rochester), Michael Rochester, among others. Jean's firesides consisted of a round of prayers, Bahá'ís and non-Bahá'ís alike taking turns. (Prayer was another thing that I didn't understand and didn't do.) Margaret Parkhill gave me my first prayer book and I started to try it. After the prayer round, Jean would provide a passage from a book like *Bahá'í World Faith* or *The Gleanings*. We would read in turns and discuss it, taking turns saying what we thought each bit meant. I always thought the meaning was clear and was always amazed at how many other facets there were. After that we broke into groups. I would browse from group to group. Last came home baked cake and tea or coffee and more good talk. It was bliss.

My mother asked me not to decide to become a Bahá'í until I was 21 years old. By now I was 18 and had even attended a couple of the summer schools at Lake Couchiching. I knew more about the Faith (technically) than some of the Bahá'ís.

I became a little older, changed my job, met a man with whom I became engaged. I had problems with him almost from the beginning and used to sometimes talk about them with my good fireside friend Charlie Grindlay, but I stopped going to the firesides and at the end of the engagement and six months, I found that I had spent all my time with him and his friends and felt that I was "on the shelf." I decided that the very first thing anybody invited me to I would accept. Immediately an invitation appeared in the mail from the Bahá'ís to a public meeting in the Kate Leonard Room, YWCA. True to my pledge, I went.

I was feeling in fine fettle, back where I belonged, and I came steaming into the room and straight up to Charlie Grindlay with both hands outstretched, saying "Look Charlie -- NO RING!"

I visited here and there and as people began to take their seats found myself one of the last still standing. I realized that the quiet man who had been standing beside Charlie when I came in was still at my elbow so we sat down together. I became extremely aware of how conscious he was of me--without his saying anything—and it made me so nervous that I became cold and shivered and all my joints snapped. Very embarrassing. He immediately went to close the window.

He is my husband of 39 years, Ben Koltermann. We remained friends with the Bahá'ís. Charlie Grindlay had become a Bahá'í and immediately pioneered to Niagara Falls. There he taught David Bowie. David's wife, Carol, also became a Bahá'í. Florence Grindlay returned from months in Scotland to find, to her dismay, her husband had become a Bahá'í--although just before she left she drew his attention to notice of a Bahá'í public meeting in the newspaper and suggested he attend because she recognized it as a Persian word. (They lived in Abadan, Iran, when Charlie worked for Anglo-Iranian oil.) Ben and I, though not Bahá'ís, were consciously instrumental in her becoming a Bahá'í. And Florence had a lot to do with our relationship not dying early on the vine through someone else's interference. The time came that they were all hard-working, devoted Bahá'ís and we were an engaged couple two weeks away from our wedding day.

That fateful day we decided that we would not be Bahá'ís. We liked the Bahá'ís and would be "fellow travelers." We were dismayed by how hard we saw our Bahá'í friends working for the Faith and we didn't want to have a life like that. We were married, and had a three day honeymoon. Then the "Hounds of Heaven" as Nancy Campbell said, began to pursue us. That is a frightening thing to live through.

We became a living legend for years in the Niagara area of what can happen when the Hounds of Heaven pursue you. (We deserved it!) In the six months it took until we had sufficiently matured to declare our Faith, we went through an incredible number of wide-ranging tests and difficulties. We didn't bring them on ourselves. They were visited upon us. As soon as we were Bahá'ís, it all stopped instantly and nothing remotely like it has ever happened again.

There was a weather-caused business failure and what would have been bankruptcy if we had been willing to declare it, but we arranged to pay our debts. There was Ben's broken nose, a cast on his leg, the apparent first case of diphtheria in 20 years in the province, almost death because of the diphtheria medication, (the Bahá'ís prayed for him, a miracle occurred and Ben, a nominal atheist became a devotedly praying person!--two miracles.) There were two vehicle accidents, neither one his fault, but which shocked me -- having always led a sheltered life. I was 20 years old, pregnant, and isolated in a tiny, diphtheria-placarded apartment with a shared bath, and warned by Ben's physician not to go out because if a child in the neighborhood should get sick, they might STONE ME IN THE STREET! Can you imagine being barely twenty years old and told something like that in Canada in 1957? Even my parents just left food on the doorstep. Only a Bahá'í insisted on coming to visit--but I forbade it. Those are really a few of the things that happened in that six month period.

At the end of the six months, Ben and I both had read *The Will and Testament of 'Abdu'l-Bahá* and written our letter to the National Spiritual Assembly stating our acceptance of it and all the other things one had to know in those days. We were invited to meet with the Regional Teaching Committee at the International Bahá'í Picnic at Queenston Heights. There we sat in their circle on the grass under the big trees and they talked with us about our becoming Bahá'ís. I remember I was already looking quite pregnant and I timorously asked them if any allowance was made for people in my condition in working for the Faith. They reassured me, I'm sure, but I was still convinced they weren't going to let me in!--because I had asked that question and wouldn't work hard enough! When they finally came from their meeting and told us that we could be Bahá'ís I burst into tears of relief and Inez Hayes, Esther's mother, held me in her arms so lovingly and comforted me.

I went home and wrote letters withdrawing from the political party, the Order of the Eastern Star (mine was also a strongly Masonic family) and the United Church of Canada.

I have never been disappointed by the Bahá'í Faith. (It sounds arrogant to say it but it completes the picture.) It has met all of my criteria, and much, much more. Our four children are all active Bahá'ís.

**Mary Thin-Koltermann**, Central Okanagan, British Columbia, Canada

# Grade School

Grade schools offer great opportunity for both students and parents to promote the Faith. To start, try to acquaint the teacher with the Faith. Have a meeting with him/her to discuss your religion. One important reason could be that you want your child not to attend school on Bahá'í Holy Days. In this meeting, you have a chance to explain a bit about the Faith, offering some literature. Follow it up by offering to clarify any points.

## *Children*

They will develop friendships with their classmates and sometimes socialize after school. They are invited to birthday parties and sleep-overs. This is a perfect chance to share Bahá'í activities, such as the Holy Days, prayers and classes.

If possible, invite your child's friends to participate in a Bahá'í function. This way they learn about the Faith without you having to talk about it. Gradually, they will know about your religion by the fact you celebrate a different New Year and different gift-giving times, as well as unique Holy Days.

## *Parents*

As a parent, you will get many opportunities to meet other parents at the school or at other child-centered activities. Over the years, with some you may develop friendships. If the timing is right, invite them to do something together as families such as a pot luck dinner at your home or a picnic at a park. Other ideas for family activities are soccer, baseball, bowling, swimming and so on. Without mentioning a word about religion, you can show your love, spirit, and attitude as freely as you want.

As a parent, your main concern is the well-being of your child, a concern shared by most other parents. Engage other parents in discussion about raising children. The Bahá'í approach is unique. If the right situation arises, share these ideas with them:

- Children are humans created in the image and likeness of God.
- Building good character is a very important part of education to the point that acquiring virtues takes precedence over academic achievements. Children are encouraged to vigorously pursue both academic and spiritual excellence.
- Education of children is seen as a vital part of the progress of mankind.

# Bahá'í Holy Days

We live in a pluralistic society and one of the important trends in the past hundred years is a growth in religious tolerance. Most countries have adopted a major religion, like Christianity in the Western Hemisphere, Hinduism in India, and Islam in the Middle East. In many of these places, there is acceptance of the practices of other religions, including the Bahá'í Faith. For example, in Canada Christianity is the main religion; there are also Jews, Buddhists, Muslims, Hindus, and Bahá'ís. By the law of the land, followers of all these religions have the right to practice their own faith. There are many Christian Holy days, and it is the right of non-Christians to ask for a day off from work or school for their holy days.

Approach your employer about the Bahá'í Holy Days. Be prepared to educate your boss with the teachings of the Faith. In countries where there is no such support by law, it is still a good idea to approach your employer with this issue. It gives you a chance to talk about the Faith. If you feel comfortable, send special gifts to work to celebrate Intercalary Days.

# Christmas Parties

Christianity is the largest religion in the world, and Christmas is its most festive time. You may be invited to parties by friends, neighbors, and colleagues. Bahá'ís may hesitate to participate because people serve alcohol, which is prohibited in our religion.

But it could be a great opportunity to meet colleagues in a social setting. When they notice you are not taking any alcohol, they may start asking questions. You can start a conversation about the Faith—not necessarily about the consumption of alcohol. You may mention why we do not participate in the commercial aspect of Christmas, although in spirit we celebrate the birth of Christ. You may also talk about our New Year and Intercalary Days. Usually at parties, people are in a relaxed mood, more likely to engage in a conversation. Be sure to avoid controversial subjects that might explode into a dispute.

# TEACHING MOMENT—A CHRISTMAS RESPONSE

Most Bahá'ís probably have a favorite way of responding during the Christmas season, when friends and acquaintances ask us if we are ready for Christmas, or if we have done all our shopping, etc. We can often turn the situation into a teaching opportunity, as we let our friends know that we, too, have special times of the year for celebration, and while we believe in the Birth of Christ and revere Him as a Manifestation of God, we do not celebrate Christmas in a commercial way.

One year after the Christmas holiday, I met an acquaintance, Robin O'Connor, when we both were picking up our children from play school. She asked me how my Christmas had been. By that time, I was quite tired of explaining to people why we didn't celebrate Christmas, and I just about said, "oh, fine." But, fortunately, I did tell her that I was a Bahá'í and that we had other times for gift-giving and commemoration. Robin was very interested, and had heard about the Faith, but had never met a Bahá'í. She began learning about it and coming to firesides, and, in time, declared her faith in Bahá'u'lláh. How glad I was that I hadn't taken the easy way out!

**Pat Verge**, Cochrane, Alberta, Canada

# Bahá'í New Year

After you have been to Christmas parties or other festive events such as Hanukkah, Divali, or Id al-Fitr (festival of the breaking of Moslem fast), it is time to show our co-workers, friends, and acquaintances how Bahá'ís have good times. A perfect occasion is our New Year (Naw-Rúz). On the first day of spring--after one Bahá'ís month of fasting--we celebrate our new year. Usually, there is a gathering in our own community or several communities get together.

It is a big event for Bahá'ís around the world and time for families and friends to get together. Although we don't drink alcohol, we can certainly have a very good time without intoxication. It is also an occasion to talk about the Bahá'í new year with people we come across during this time. Living in a pluralistic society, we are accustomed to other New Years, such as Christian, Jewish, Chinese, and Indian. Talking about ours should not be in the least bit strange.

# Friends

After accepting the message of Bahá'u'lláh, you might have two extreme feelings towards your friends. One is that you can't wait to tell them about its greatness, and its teachings about the soul, the purpose of life, the solution of the problems of the world, and its great vision for mankind. On the other hand, you may worry about how your friends will react towards your new religion. Therefore, you may hesitate to talk about it, fearing the risk of losing their friendship. Or, you share bits and pieces over a long period of time. Trying to hide will not help; eventually, they will discover you are going to Feasts and possessed by strange ideas like the unity of mankind, world government, prayer, meditation, justice, and so on.

Regardless of the approach, we do give a lot of thought as to how to give this precious message to our friends. Knowing its goodness, we dearly wish they could see the way we do.

One has to be prepared for the reaction of friends. It might be the opposite of what we expected. If it is positive, then everything is fine. But the reaction will often vary from luke-warm to no response. In this case, we have to exercise patience, as each one of us is in total control of our own spiritual destiny. Saying prayers, and reassuring them of your friendship would also help.

Remember, many of us have become Bahá'ís through friends. The trust and love that already exist make it safer for a friend to seriously consider your spiritual path.

# Family Members

Like your friends, you want to share the message with your family members: parents, brothers, sisters, spouse, and children. This could be one of the most exciting, yet challenging teaching moments of your life. It is a great blessing when other members of the family join the Faith. For assistance, here is a beautiful prayer:

Glory be unto Thee, O Lord my God! I beg Thee to forgive me and those who support Thy Faith. Verily, Thou art the sovereign Lord, the Forgiver, the Most Generous. O my God! Enable such servants of Thine as are deprived of knowledge to be admitted into Thy Cause; for once they learn of Thee, they bear witness to the truth of the Day of Judgement and do not dispute the revelations of Thy bounty. Send down upon them the tokens of Thy grace, and grant them, wherever they reside, a liberal share of that which Thou hast ordained for the pious among Thy servants. Thou art in truth the Supreme Ruler, the All-Bounteous, the Most Benevolent.

O my God! Let the outpourings of Thy bounty and blessings descend upon homes whose inmates have embraced Thy Faith, as a token of Thy grace and as a mark of loving-kindness from Thy presence. Verily, unsurpassed art Thou in granting forgiveness. Should Thy bounty be withheld from anyone, how could he be reckoned among the followers of the Faith in Thy Day?

Bless me, O my God, and those who will believe in Thy signs on the appointed Day, and such as cherish my love in their hearts—a love which Thou dost instill into them. Verily, Thou art the Lord of righteousness, the Most Exalted.
   (**The Báb**, *Bahá'í Prayers*, p. 63)

 # Word Check

| pious | 1. devout in religion. |
|-------|------------------------|
|       | 2. ostentatiously virtuous. |
| **benevolent** | wishing to do good to others, kindly, and helpful. |
| **outpouring** | spoken and written expression of emotion. |

There is no doubt we want our family members to benefit from the message of Bahá'u'lláh. Often, many family members join, but if your efforts don't seem to be fruitful, remember that each soul progresses at its own rate; therefore, some do take a bit longer time than others. It is also important to maintain unity in the family.

The next few paragraphs give a few ideas of how to teach family members.

## Parents

In most parts of the world, the child follows the religion of the parent. Joining a new religion with a foreign-sounding name can cause a lot of anxiety for parents. For lack of information, some think the Bahá'í Faith is a cult. There is fear that a feeble mind can be a victim of domination and deceit. Many times anxieties are well founded, based on real fears of mind control. Many have joined cults and consequently have experienced personal disaster.

Changing religion can be taken as abandoning family traditions and seen as a disgrace. Therefore, it is important to acquaint parents with the principles and laws of the Faith. Sometimes they have a favorable response; one should also be prepared for adverse reactions.

It may be unthinkable that parents would adopt the children's new-found religion, but it has happened on many occasions. One should not give up hope but continue to teach parents with diligence and wisdom. Here are prayers for parents revealed by The Báb and 'Abdu'l-Bahá.

I beg Thy forgiveness, O my God, and implore pardon after the manner Thou wishest Thy servants to direct themselves to Thee. I beg of Thee to wash away our sins as befitteth Thy Lordship, and to forgive me, my parents, and those who in Thy estimation have entered the abode of Thy love in a manner which is worthy of Thy transcendent sovereignty and well beseemeth the glory of Thy celestial power.

O my God! Thou hast inspired my soul to offer its supplication to Thee, and but for Thee, I would not call upon Thee. Lauded and glorified art Thou; I yield Thee praise inasmuch as Thou didst reveal Thyself unto me, and I beg Thee to forgive me, since I have fallen short in my duty to know Thee and have failed to walk in the path of Thy love.

**(The Báb**, *Bahá'í Prayers*, p. 64)

O Lord! In this Most Great Dispensation Thou dost accept the intercession of children in behalf of

their parents. This is one of the special infinite
bestowals of this Dispensation. Therefore, O Thou
kind Lord, accept the request of this Thy servant
at the threshold of Thy singleness and submerge
his father in the ocean of Thy grace, because this
son hath arisen to render Thee service and is
exerting effort at all times in the pathway of Thy
love. Verily, Thou art the Giver, the Forgiver and
the Kind!

('**Abdu'l-Bahá**, *Bahá'í Prayers*, p. 65)

 # Word Check

| diligence | done with care and effort. |
|---|---|
| transcendent | going beyond the limits of ordinary experience, surpassing. |
| beseem | to be fitting or seemly. |
| supplication | to ask humbly for, to beseech. |
| intercession | to intervene on behalf of another person. |
| submerge | to dive, to go below the surface. |
| exerting | making a great effort. |

## Siblings

It would be a natural step to share the banquet of good news of the Bahá'í Faith with those very close to you, especially your brothers and sisters. You will know your siblings well and how to present the Faith in the most appropriate ways:

- Let them know about your new Faith and the reasons for joining.
- Offer literature, either of a general nature or related to their particular areas of interest.
- One should be careful about making assumptions when introducing your siblings to the Faith. Ensure that the same serious attention is given as would be to a stranger.

Many have become Bahá'ís through the teaching efforts of siblings.

## Spouse

There is always a strong desire to share the Faith with a spouse who is not a Bahá'í. One can also understand—given the close relationship between two persons—that one could become anxious for the other person to join the Faith and enjoy together many aspects of Bahá'í life. But, one should always be mindful of the fact that difference of religious beliefs or not giving the other partner adequate time to investigate his/her own spiritual path, may potentially break up the marriage. Here is a prayer:

> As to thy respected husband: it is incumbent upon thee to treat him with great kindness, to consider his wishes and be conciliatory with him at all times, till he seeth that because thou hast directed thyself toward the Kingdom of God, thy tenderness for him and thy love for God have but increased, as well thy concern for his wishes under all conditions.
> (**Abdu'l-Bahá**, *Selections from the Writings of 'Abdu'l-Bahá*, p. 122)

> O God, my God! This Thy handmaid is calling upon

Thee, trusting in Thee, turning her face unto Thee, imploring Thee to shed Thy heavenly bounties upon her, and to disclose unto her Thy spiritual mysteries, and to cast upon her the lights of Thy Godhead.

O my Lord! Make the eyes of my husband to see. Rejoice Thou his heart with the light of the knowledge of Thee, draw Thou his mind unto Thy luminous beauty, cheer Thou his Spirit by revealing unto him Thy manifest splendors.

O my Lord! Lift Thou the veil from before his sight. Rain down Thy plenteous bounties upon him, intoxicate him with the wine of love for Thee, make him one of Thy angels whose feet walk upon this earth even as their souls are soaring through the high heavens. Cause him to become a brilliant lamp, shining out with the light of Thy wisdom in the midst of Thy people.

Verily, Thou are the Precious, the Ever-Bestowing, the Open of Hand.
   (**'Abdu'l-Bahá**, *Bahá'í Prayers, p. 65*)

# Word Check

| conciliatory | overcome the anger or hostility of, to win the goodwill of. |
|---|---|
| tenderness | loving and gentle. |
| imploring | requesting earnestly, to entreat. |
| plenteous | plentiful. |
| intoxicate | excite or exhilarate beyond self-control. |

## Children

Teaching the Faith to one's children is one of the most challenging and important tasks in promoting the Faith. In fact, one of Bahá'u'lláh's commandments is that Bahá'í children be raised to recognize God and His Manifestations, as stated in these words:

> Marry, O people, that from you may appear he who will remember Me amongst My servants; this is one of My commandments unto you; obey it as an assistance to yourselves.
>
> (**Bahá'u'lláh**, *Bahá'í Prayers*, p. 105)

These words are potent and it seems for a Bahá'í parent that the success of parenting depends on our children accepting God and joining the Faith. There is always the nagging concern of how our children will progress in life. Each child is so unique and there are so many factors—both good and bad—that can contribute to his/her development that it is impossible to predict the final outcome.

Many parents wonder if there is a sure-fire method that would make every Bahá'í child a believer. And teaching the Bahá'í Faith to our children is more important—we are accountable to God about this duty—than bringing someone else to the Faith. Growing up in a Bahá'í family does not necessarily guarantee one will believe in Bahá'u'lláh. But with a conscientious effort in providing the right family and spiritual atmosphere and special individual care, one would hope the child would recognize the truth in the Bahá'í Message. To help with this challenging task of teaching our offspring, here are few suggestions:

- If your children are young, give them religious education by sending them to Bahá'í school.
- Give them a Bahá'í identity by allowing them to participate in Bahá'í schools, Feasts, etc.
- Family activities: prayers, stories, summer schools.
- Let them know about your belief system. Young minds are very inquisitive and ask all kinds of questions about many things they observe. It is a great opportunity to explain realities according to the Bahá'í teachings.

 ## TEACHING MOMENT—A PRACTICAL JOKER

When Doris Kettle lived in Lakefield, Ontario, Canada, they had a neighbor who was a bit of a practical joker. Doris was always looking for a religion that made sense. She would constantly invite into her home the Jehovah Witnesses, the Mormons, and any others that would knock at her door trying to share the truth.

Doris was an avid reader and had a library with a variety of books to challenge the best of readers.

This neighbor knew about this, and as a joke, she told a Bahá'í, Gladys Garbutt, that Doris was interested in the Bahá'í Faith. Both lived on the same street. The neighbor also knew Doris had never heard about the Faith. Not knowing about this, Gladys courageously knocked on the Kettles' door and was very embarrassed when Doris told her that she had not sent for her and had never heard of the Bahá'í Faith. Doris, in her quest for truth, did not want to let this opportunity pass by. Therefore, she invited Gladys in to tell her about this unheard of religion.

It did not take long for Doris to become a Bahá'í and get excited about it. Very soon, her husband, Douglas, and daughters, Heather, Ann, and Bonnie, all joined the new religion.

**Maddie Wingett**, Peterborough, Ontario, Canada

# Ethnic Groups

Migration of people from one country to another has happened at a phenomenal rate in this century, making our societies of this planet more diverse than ever, both racially and culturally. For various reasons, one pattern that has emerged is that ethnic groups in pluralistic societies have very little cultural contact with each other. For example, there is no cultural exchange among the Germans, Turks, Italians, and Portuguese in Germany, or the French, African, and Arabs in France, or the Jews, Africans, Polish, and Latinos in the USA, or the Natives, English, and French in Canada. These are just a few examples, but this ethnic isolation is widespread throughout the world.

But one thing common among any of these groups is that they are proud of their heritage. They would like to share it with anyone who is interested. One of the most beautiful teachings of the Bahá'í Faith is preservation of ethnic cultures.

Like the different shapes and colors of flowers that contribute to the beauty of the garden, cultures are essential parts of the magnificent garden of humanity. Many people are so eager to share their ways of life, that all you have to do is ask them about their food, beliefs, costumes, cultures, and so on. You will be surprised how much they want to share. In return, you will get a chance to tell about your heritage. The social contact will bring more appreciation of each other's culture, leading to more harmony in our multicultural societies.

Newcomers to a new country tend to gravitate towards a group from their native land. We have this happen in the Bahá'í world. The reasons are obvious. Establishing oneself in a new country means going through many changes. Ethnic subcultures are a taste of the old country. Ethnic associations are sources of comfort to friends while they cope with the changes. These mini cultural centers in many parts of the world brought about by the movement of immigrants give the Bahá'ís a great opportunity to celebrate the diversity of the human race right in our "own backyard."

To the gatherings, such as New Year, conferences, and so on, invite an ethnic group in your neighborhood to present their dances and music. This could be Portuguese, Africans, Polish, Indian, Irish or Scottish cultural association. This will give you a chance to inform them of the Faith as well as promote harmony, which is badly needed.

# TEACHING MOMENT—A BAHÁ'Í ALL MY LIFE

In a sense, I have been a Bahá'í all my life without hearing about the prophet Bahá'u'lláh. The principles and laws I have believed since I was young. In 1991, I heard an interview of Jarna and John Milne on Asian Television, Toronto,

Canada. It intensified my curiosity. I was impressed and I said to myself I should pursue this further. I was impressed with the aspect of independent search for the truth. Probably by then I had just heard the name Bahá'í. Finding the truth for myself is very important to me. And not following blindly the priest or forefathers. I was born in New Delhi, India. It was in Toronto that I encountered the Faith. I was brought up in the Sikh religion of my parents but I did not like certain dogmas and rituals. People worship many icons and deities and it did not sit well with me. If there is a merciful God, He is the Father of all. The vision that man creates that "my religion is better than yours" is a conflict in my mind. To me it is not the way of finding the truth.

First I got the phone number of the Milne from the TV interview. John and Jarna Milne invited me to their home and we had a discussion of the Faith. After that there has been no turning back. I pursued it with earnestness. I was hooked for good. I started going to the Bahá'í book store almost every Sunday night. I borrowed books to study. The more I learned about this new religion the more enchanted I became.

What really impressed me was the universal application of the Faith. The independent search for truth, the salvation of mankind and transformation of society. I did not exactly believe in God. Although I was brought up in the Sikh religion, I turned agnostic for most of my life. All my life I believed in Darwin's theory of evolution. Creation and evolution were big subjects in my mind.

After eight months of study and regularly going to firesides at the Milnes' home, one day John asked me, "Kam, what are you waiting for, why are you sitting on the fence?" I replied, "I want to be 110 percent sure, let me study further. Let me do some more research. It is like a life long marriage to me. I have to be very sure."

He said, "Kam, you can first declare and do your research after."

I said, "Yeah, it make sense, why not?"

That evening I declared and there has been no turning back. Six months later my wife, Vibha, joined too.

**Kam Singh**, Toronto, Ontario, Canada

# Organizations

After you have explored all the opportunities previously discussed and you are still looking for more ways to contact people, there is one great avenue: organizations.

Organizations such as clubs and special interest groups are great places of meeting people who have common interests. And there is one for almost any imaginable subject—from insects to space travel, Elvis Fan Club to poetry, and from meditation to computers. Local papers are the place to find the group you are looking for. The local library can be of some help, as can local information centers or town/city agencies.

There are often community groups working in social development issues of great interest to Bahá'ís, such as eliminating racism, promoting women's development, environmental and human rights issues. Bahá'ís can often bring perspectives that elevate the work to the level of principle and help promote real social change. Training courses in social and economic development will assist Bahá'í communities to become increasingly involved and effective in this work.

Involvement in such groups will take care of an interest in your life and help you meet people of similar goals. This will help promote friendship and trust, which can eventually lead to sharing of the Bahá'í Faith.

# Religious Groups

One of the great forces of the Bahá'í Revelation is its ability to bring about religious harmony. We have the knowledge and attitudes that can promote this goal. To start, make a list of religious groups, such as Christianity, Buddhism, Judaism, Hinduism, Islam, and so on. You may want to include groups that do not have a religious affiliation but are spiritually inclined such as a prayer or meditation group.

You may attend their activities and when appropriate let them know you are a Bahá'í. Sometimes you may get a cold response; they may think you are there to steal their membership. On the other hand, you may find like-minded souls, who are not necessarily interested in converting one another but working on common concerns, for example, prayer for world peace or helping the poor in the neighborhood. There are also many new groups promoting interfaith dialogue to which you can make a meaningful contribution.

# More Opportunities

So far we have looked at some of the places to find souls to teach. Actually, these are only a few of the many ways of finding opportunities. Some may need consultation with a Local Spiritual Assembly to avoid conflict or duplication. If you have doubts approach a Bahá'í Institution, like the Local Assembly or the assistant to the Auxiliary Board member. Here is a list of teaching ideas:

- Offer Bahá'í books to public, school, university libraries. By contacting the local media, there is a possibility of getting publicity for your donation.
- Prepare a course on the Bahá'í Faith or comparative religion, and offer it to high schools, college extension departments, churches, and any other groups.
- Share Bahá'í news with friends and acquaintances. It could be local events or developments in the Bahá'í World.
- Send Bahá'í postcards to friends and relatives.
- Give copies of *God Loves Laughter* to your doctor.

- Offer an introductory course on the Faith to the general public.

# Summary

So far, we have discussed many ways of meeting souls to whom talking about the Faith is a possibility. This is just a short list; there are many more ways to find waiting souls. One of the most important aspects of teaching is to have the Name of Bahá'u'lláh known to everyone we come in contact with as a top priority. If it is not in the forefront of our minds, sometimes opportunities may be missed.

Be careful, impatience and anxiety may distract you from naturally leading to the right subjects. You can create the opportunities by steering your conversation to common subjects which are related to the Bahá'í Faith. Directly or indirectly, you can always express the Bahá'í point of view.

# TEACHING BREAK

THERE IS SUCH THING AS A <u>BAD</u> TIME TO TEACH

# 5

# The Message

Bahá'u'lláh came to earth in the station of Prophethood with the sole purpose of delivering to mankind a divine Message inspired by the Holy Spirit. The amount of revelation was voluminous, recorded over a 40 years period. This Message was not like any other; it is a charter for the development of life on this planet for at least the next 900 years. He wrote on various subjects that influence human lives such as the purpose of life, spiritual and social principles, laws governing communities, marriage, education, science, religion, world government, and many more. Now all His precious words are in the hands of Bahá'ís to be delivered to the rest of humanity.

As valuable as we think the message of Bahá'u'lláh is, it is not always easy for others to accept it the way we do. Our teaching experience shows that people do not always receive it the way a thirsty one would snatch a glass of water, although some prepared souls have embraced it the moment they heard. For the masses it will require skillful teachers to successfully deliver this divine message. In this chapter, we will discuss many aspects of delivering the Bahá'í message, namely:

- The Approach
- What to say
- The right message
- The power of words
- How to say it

- Message
- Method
- Examples

# The Approach

We understand that Bahá'u'lláh's message is not only beneficial to ourselves but to others. Our duty, prescribed by the Prophet, is to deliver it as a gift from Him to others. Bahá'ís are His messengers, but He added a condition to this request: *how we deliver the message is as important as the message.* This is a deviation from the past. In previous dispensations, violence and coercion were allowed in order to convert people to a new religion. But, in this Dispensation both are absolutely prohibited.

According to Bahá'u'lláh, we must be equipped with divine qualities, and not with weapons, for the message to affect others. He explains this clearly in these words:

> O Friends! You must all be so ablaze in this day **with the fire of the love of God** that the heat thereof may be manifest in all your veins, your limbs and members of your body, and the peoples of the world may be ignited by this heat and turn to the horizon of the Beloved.
> (**Bahá'u'lláh**, *The Individual and Teaching*, p. 3)

> If ye be aware of a certain truth...of which others are deprived, share it with them in a **language of utmost kindliness and good-will**...If any one should refuse it, leave him unto himself, and beseech God to guide him.
> (**Bahá'u'lláh**, *The Individual and Teaching*, p. 4)

...show forth, when conversing with him, a spirit
of **extreme kindliness and good-will**. Help him to
see and recognize the truth, without esteeming
yourself to be, in the least, superior to him, or
to be possessed of greater endowments.
(**Bahá'u'lláh**, *The Individual and Teaching*, p. 4)

In Chapter One, we looked at love as being an essential ingredient in teaching. According to Bahá'u'lláh, other qualities such as kindness and goodwill are also important. Here are more necessary qualities according to 'Abdu'l-Bahá:

If thou wishest to guide the souls, it is incumbent
on thee to be **firm**, to be **good** and to be imbued
with **praiseworthy attributes** and **divine qualities**
under all circumstances. Be a sign of **love**, a
manifestation of **mercy**, a foundation of **tenderness**,
**kindhearted**, **good** to all and **gentle** to the servants
of God...
(**Bahá'u'lláh**, *The Individual and Teaching*, p. 10)

The teacher, when teaching, must be himself fully
enkindled, so that his utterance, like unto a flame
of fire, may exert influence and consume the veil
of self and passion. He must also be utterly **humble**
and **lowly**, so that others may be edified and be
totally **self-effaced** and **evanescent** so that he may
teach with the melody of the Concourse on
high—otherwise his teaching will have no effect.
(**'Abdu'l-Bahá**, *The Individual and Teaching*, p. 10)

The aim is this: The intention of the teacher must
be **pure**, his heart **independent**, his spirit
**attracted**, his **thought at peace**, his **resolution
firm**, his **magnanimity exalted** and in the **love of
God** a shining torch. Should he become as such, his

sanctified breath will even affect the rock;
otherwise there will be no result whatsoever.

('**Abdu'l-Bahá**, *Tablets of the Divine Plan*, revealed on April 19, 20 and 22,
1916, p. 20)

 # Word Check

| | |
|---|---|
| **kindliness** | kind in character or manner or appearance. |
| **goodwill** | a friendly feeling. |
| **endowments** | power or ability or quality. |
| **incumbent** | forming an obligation or duty. |
| **kindhearted** | having a kind heart, sympathetic to others. |
| **self-effaced** | tending to avoid the notice of others, humble. |
| **evanescent** | fading quickly. |
| **resolution** | a mental pledge, something one intends to do. |
| **magnanimity** | noble and generous in one's conduct, not petty. |
| **sanctify** | to make holy or sacred. |

The following lists the qualities of Bahá'í teachers mentioned in *The Individual and Teaching*.

| | | |
|---|---|---|
| enkindled | righteous | detached |
| kind | dedicated | friendly |
| selfless | upright | praiseworthy |
| pure | attracted | loving |
| firm | persevering | determined |
| persistent | eloquent | confident |
| assured | wise | self-sacrificing |
| merciful | good | humble |
| tender | courageous | tolerant |
| patient | truthful | understanding |
| consecrated | loyal | passionate |
| tactful | prayerful | devoted |
| enthusiastic | hopeful | cheerful |
| happy | faithful | prejudice-free |
| hospitable | audacious | |

# What to Say

Over the years, as our faith becomes firmer, we acquire more knowledge and understanding about the principles, guidance, and laws of the Bahá'í Faith. Often we get this feeling: "If I could only understand more, it would be easier to teach." So, when informing someone about the Faith, there is a great tendency to tell it all to whoever has a few moments to listen. Or, if we are utterly impressed by some aspect, for example, the infallibility of the Universal House of Justice, unity of mankind or world government, there is a tendency to speak about what is *our* consuming interest with others. Unfortunately, it may not be *their* interest and we must avoid the temptation of dumping so much information as to baffle a would-be-Bahá'í. On the contrary, a teacher has to gauge the needs and deliver the message in the right dosage.

Consider a professor. This person may be knowledgeable about many subjects. At the first lecture of the class—or any other time—it would not be appropriate to the students to speak about all his or her favorite subjects. It would make the audience totally confused. Rather, it would be wise to follow strictly a curriculum for that particular class. During another class, the professor may discuss entirely different subjects appropriate to the audience.

Let's look at another analogy. A doctor will not prescribe medicine as soon as someone walks into his office. A good practitioner will first listen to the patient's illness and then offer a medicine accordingly.

As teachers of the Bahá'í Faith, we have to cultivate the skills of both the professor and the doctor. Like the professor, we impart knowledge and, like the doctor, we give the right spiritual medicine. According to 'Abdu'l-Bahá, we must:

> First diagnose the disease and identify the malady, then prescribe the remedy...
>
> (**'Abdu'l-Bahá**, *The Individual and Teaching*, p. 13)

# The Right Message

Saying the right thing is not always easy. How can you give the appropriate message to someone just by talking for a few minutes? Even if you know someone for a long time, it is hard to understand the inner state of a soul the way 'Abdu'l-Bahá did. What makes one tick? What is the spiritual food one needs?

Bahá'u'lláh understands this problem very well and resolved it in the following way:

> Proclaim, then, that which **the Most Great Spirit will inspire thee** *to utter* in the service of the Cause of thy Lord, that thou mayest stir up the souls of all men and incline their hearts unto this most blessed and all-glorious Court...
> **(Bahá'u'lláh**, *Gleanings from the Writings of Bahá'u'lláh*, p. 303)

This is a guarantee given only to teachers of the Faith and not to doctors or professors. This assistance is always--seven days a week and twenty-four hours a day—available to any one of us. All we have to do is lean on it. In this important work, we are not alone; we have the greatest help imaginable.

One of the advantages of this method is that a thorough knowledge of the Faith is not absolutely required. The proof of this is that in the early days of the Faith, most believers did not possess all the materials that we have today, yet fearlessly they spiritually conquered many continents. It happens all the time—how many times have we heard teachers of the Faith say: "I said so many things, and I don't know where they came from."

# The Power of Words

Another important aspect of stirring up the souls is the use of the Holy Words as much as possible. They are endowed with potent forces. Bahá'u'lláh explains:

From the texts of the wondrous, heavenly Scriptures they should memorize phrases and passages bearing on various instances, so that in the course of their speech they may recite divine verses whenever the occasion demandeth it, inasmuch as these holy verses are the most potent elixir, the greatest and mightiest talisman. So potent is their influence that the hearer will have no cause for vacillation.
   (**Bahá'u'lláh**, *Tables of Bahá'u'lláh*, p. 200)

The Word of God is the king of words and its pervasive influence is incalculable...The Word is the master key for the whole world.
   (**Bahá'u'lláh**, *Tablets of Bahá'u'lláh*, p. 173)

As well, we cannot underestimate the influence of human words. As seen earlier, they must be wrapped in extreme goodwill and kindness, to supplement the positive effect of the Holy Words. Otherwise, unfriendly words can leave a bad taste.

## Word Check

| diagnose | make a statement of the nature of a disease or other condition after observing its signs and symptoms. |
|---|---|
| prescribe | to lay down as a course or rule to be followed. |
| stir | to arouse or excite or stimulate. |
| elixir | 1. a fragrant liquid used as a medicine or flavoring.<br>2. a remedy believed to cure all ills. |
| talisman | an object supposed to bring good luck. |
| vacillation | 1. waver, to keep changing one's mind.<br>2. to swing or sway unsteadily. |

## The Message

Inspiration is a key part of teaching, but knowing what Bahá'u'lláh has said about various aspects of life will only help you further. It will make you more knowledgeable and confident. Giving the actual Words of the Manifestation is very important as they have special powers attached to each one of them that can affect a soul more than our own. Of course, when the Words are not at the tip of our tongue, we can use the next best thing: paraphrasing.

The following is a list of some of the subjects extracted from the Bahá'í Writings that may help you.

## God

Thou hast asked regarding the phrase, 'He is God!' written above the Tablets. By this Word it is intended that no one hath any access to the Invisible Essence. The way is barred and the road is impassable. In this world all men must turn their faces toward 'Him-whom-God-shall-Manifest'. He is the 'Dawning-place of Divinity' and the 'Manifestation of Deity'. He is the 'Ultimate Goal', the 'Adored One' of all and the 'Worshiped One' of all. Otherwise, whatever flashes through the mind is not that Essence of essences and the Reality of realities; nay, rather it is pure imagination woven by man and is surrounded, not the surrounding. Consequently, it returns finally to the realm of suppositions and conjectures.

('**Abdu'l-Bahá**, *Tablets of 'Abdu'l-Bahá*, pp. 513-514)

As the divine entity is eternal, the divine attributes are co-existent, co-eternal. The divine bestowals are therefore without beginning, without end. God is infinite; the works of God are infinite; the bestowals of God are infinite. As His divinity is eternal, His lordship and perfections are without end. As the bounty of the Holy Spirit is eternal, we can never say that His bestowals terminate, else He terminates.

('**Abdu'l-Bahá**, *Foundations of World Unity*, p. 102)

## Prophet or Manifestation

God hath raised up Prophets and revealed Books as

numerous as the creatures of the world, and will continue to do so to everlasting.

(**The Báb**, *Selections from the Writings of the Báb*, p. 125)

The sages aforetime acquired their knowledge from the Prophets, inasmuch as the latter were the Exponents of divine philosophy and the Revealers of heavenly mysteries. Men quaffed the crystal, living waters of Their utterance, while others satisfied themselves with the dregs. Everyone receiveth a portion according to his measure.

(**Bahá'u'lláh**, *Tablets of Bahá'u'lláh*, pp. 144-145)

## Purpose of Religions

Religion bestoweth upon man the most precious of all gifts, offereth the cup of prosperity, imparteth eternal life, and showereth imperishable benefits upon mankind.

(**Bahá'u'lláh**, *Tablets of Bahá'u'lláh*, p. 130)

The religion of God is for love and unity; make it not the cause of enmity or dissension.

(**Bahá'u'lláh**, *Tablets of Bahá'u'lláh*, p. 220)

## Humanity

He Who is your Lord, the All-Merciful, cherisheth in His heart the desire of beholding the entire human race as one soul and one body.

(**Bahá'u'lláh**, *Gleanings from the Writings of Bahá'u'lláh*, p. 214)

... and human happiness consists only in drawing
closer to the Threshold of Almighty God, and in
securing the peace and well-being of every
individual member, high and low alike, of the human
race.

('**Abdu'l-Bahá**, *The Secret of Divine Civilization*, p. 60)

## Soul

...Know thou that every soul is fashioned after the
nature of God, each being pure and holy at his
birth. Afterwards, however, the individuals will
vary according to what they acquire of virtues or
vices in this world.

('**Abdu'l-Bahá**, *Selections from the Writings of 'Abdu'l-Bahá*, p. 190)

## Separation of Body and Soul

Know thou of a truth that the soul, after its
separation from the body, will continue to progress
until it attaineth the presence of God...

(**Bahá'u'lláh**, *Gleanings from the Writings of Bahá'u'lláh*, p. 155)

## Equality

...As for what is meant by the equality of souls in
the all-highest realm, it is this: the souls of the
believers, at the time when they first become
manifest in the world of the body, are equal, and
each is sanctified and pure. In this world,
however, they will begin to differ one from

another, some achieving the highest station, some a middle one, others remaining at the lowest stage of being. Their equal status is at the beginning of their existence; the differentiation followeth their passing away.

('**Abdu'l-Bahá**, *Selections from the Writings of 'Abdu'l-Bahá*, p. 171)

## Education

...The education and training of children is among the most meritorious acts of humankind and draweth down the grace and favor of the All-Merciful, for education is the indispensable foundation of all human excellence and alloweth man to work his way to the heights of abiding glory.

('**Abdu'l-Bahá**, *Selections from the Writings of 'Abdu'l-Bahá*, p. 129)

The Pen of Glory counselleth everyone regarding the instruction and education of children. Behold that which the Will of God hath revealed upon Our arrival in the Prison City and recorded in the Most Holy Book.

(**Bahá'u'lláh**, *Tablets of Bahá'u'lláh*, p. 128)

## Science and Arts

It is permissible to study sciences and arts, but such sciences as are useful and would redound to the progress and advancement of the people...

(**Bahá'u'lláh**, *Tablets of Bahá'u'lláh*, p. 26)

## *Unity*

...The purpose of justice is the appearance of unity among men.
   (**Bahá'u'lláh**, *Tablets of Bahá'u'lláh*, p. 67)

O ye men of wisdom among nations! Shut your eyes to estrangement, then fix your gaze upon unity. Cleave tenaciously unto that which will lead to the well-being and tranquillity of all mankind.
   (**Bahá'u'lláh**, *Tablets of Bahá'u'lláh*, p. 67)

...From the beginning of time the light of unity hath shed its divine radiance upon the world, and the greatest means for the promotion of that unity is for the peoples of the world to understand one another's writing and speech.
   (**Bahá'u'lláh**, *Tablets of Bahá'u'lláh*, p.127)

# Word Check

| supposition | supposing, what is supposed, *the article is based on supposition not on fact.* |
|---|---|
| conjecture | to guess. |
| bestowal | gift. |
| exponents | 1. a person who sets out the facts or interprets something.<br>2. one who favors a particular theory or policy. |
| dregs | 1. bits of worthless matter that sink to the bottom of a liquid.<br>2. the worst and useless part, *the dregs of society.* |

# TEACHING MOMENT—NO TIME TO WASTE

In September 1986, Elsie Kelly called for information about the Bahá'í Faith as a result of the advertisement placed in the local paper. The very first thing she said was, "Before I waste any of your time or mine, I want to know if the Bahá'ís believe that all mankind is the same all over the world?" I was in such a shock that I couldn't even answer for a few seconds. She began to come to firesides and soon she declared her faith in Bahá'u'lláh. She is a great volunteer in the city, always working for the homeless and underprivileged.

**Maddie Wingett**, Peterborough, Ontario, Canada

# Methods of Delivery

Once someone asked 'Abdu'l-Bahá how many methods there are of teaching. He replied that there are as many methods as there are souls. It is so true; the way you teach is slightly different for each one simply because each soul has different needs. In a way, it is like raising children. One method does not satisfy every newborn.

There are many methods that are used which can be classified into several different categories. The important point is to pick or devise one with which you are most comfortable. Equally important is not to discourage someone who has chosen a method that you don't like. For example, not everyone would choose door-to-door teaching. Yet some are very successful with this method. In some parts of the world, it is common for Bahá'ís to go from home to home in a village or town to visit and talk about the message of Bahá'u'lláh. In another case, one may do very well on a one-to-one basis, but not be up to the task of giving a fireside.

The categories discussed are:

- One-to-one teaching
- Firesides
- Public Talks
- Direct Teaching
- Mass Teaching
- Door-to-door Teaching
- Traveling Teaching
- Pioneering

## One-to-one Teaching

Every form of teaching is really reduced to a one-to-one spiritual relationship between a Bahá'í and one who is interested in the Bahá'í message. Of all the categories, this one is the most important. Usually it is some quality that you have that attracts the seeking soul. It could be something like a smile, the way you talk, confidence, trust, spirit, radiance or love. These qualities—sometimes unnoticed by you—may be the catalyst that invites others to hear the message.

The following sections discuss some of the common ways Bahá'ís around the world use to share the message of Bahá'u'lláh.

## Firesides

Holding a fireside means inviting friends or strangers to a home for the purpose of talking about the Faith in a hospitable atmosphere. In the 1940's, as the name suggests, many Bahá'ís in North America held discussions around a fireplace, creating a cozy ambience. But at the equator, the word fireside is an oxymoron. The word fireside has taken on a fuller meaning—a meeting in a home to share information, build social ties and generate new understanding through productive discussions.

The Guardian strongly believed in firesides, often encouraging friends to organize them. They are the most effective places to show love, fellowship, and spirit to potential Bahá'ís. As seen throughout this book, these are the key ingredients to success in propagating the Faith.

Firesides are held throughout the world and regardless of the place, they have been one of the best mediums for teaching. Most of us can remember either holding or attending a few. My most memorable one was held at the Laura Davis home, 44 Chestnut Park, Toronto, Canada. After two decades I have no difficulty remembering the address—it is engraved in my memory. Every Friday for decades, Laura held a fireside.

The format was simple yet very attractive. As her guests arrived, Laura would greet them with the kind of joy usually reserved for long-lost friends. Everyone was ushered into a comfortable room full of antique furniture. Then she would welcome everyone and introduce herself and her guests. Many times there would be a guest speaker who talked on a specific subject. Other times Laura would discuss topical issues. The format was free and informal so that everyone could participate. Present were Bahá'ís and those who had interest in the Faith. Some came regularly and others were just passing through, or were there until their spiritual thirst was quenched. There could be few guests or many, and always they were from a great diversity of background. The discussions were frank and open, and the spirit always high. For many Bahá'ís, it was a place to go on Friday night, where one could meet old friends and make new ones.

Towards the end of the evening, Laura directed us to another room with a long table. We sat around while she would serve tea and coffee with the greatest delight. The discussion continued until everyone left.

She had this fireside for many decades until illness prevented her from continuing it. Laura dedicated her home so that the sweetness of Bahá'u'lláh's message could be tasted. Everyone felt spiritually enriched after attending her firesides. While she did not have any physical children of her own, she saw many spiritual births in her home.

Laura's firesides were not unique. In fact, Bahá'ís around the world have such meetings all the time. Anyone can start one. However, many have been discouraged because no one showed up. This is a common problem and here is how Joe Wiseman resolved it.

He move to Toronto in 1977. Being a new Bahá'í full of spirit and energy, he organized a fireside at his apartment every Monday—the only evening he was free from work. He announced this event at the Feast and directly informed many of his friends. Many Mondays came and went while he waited for someone to come through his door to hear about the Faith. He was a bit discouraged, sad and low-spirited. After some reflection he decided to give it another chance by taking two specific steps. First he asked for unseen help through prayers and meditation. He knew it was available to him—the Concourse on High was waiting to serve him—he just had to ask. Second, he made concerted efforts to find souls who were ready to hear the message. He called all his friends and talked to people everywhere—at work, on the bus, in parks and even in restaurants. He was very determined to make it a success. Very soon, he had people coming to his firesides. Gradually, the number in attendance started to grow. Every Monday evening, Joe's tiny apartment was packed with people; though he possessed very little furniture, everyone felt very comfortable and kept coming back. Within a few months, several people declared their belief in Bahá'u'lláh.

## Public Talks

Public speaking is for the brave ones. The world has produced many great speakers, including Bahá'ís, to whom one can listen for a long time. They are both enjoyable and informative. Good speakers master this skill through long practice and preparation. Five minutes of speech may take hours of preparation.

In the Bahá'í Faith, we always need public speakers. They serve a very useful purpose by addressing a large number of people at one time. We need to bring people to the Cause in large numbers. We should not only admire their efforts, but encourage them in their endeavors.

If you are considering public speaking, it is not enough just to know the Faith well, rather you have to focus on a particular subject and expand on it for an allotted time, say ten, fifteen, or thirty minutes. To improve in this area, one can benefit by studying the speeches of the Master when He was traveling in the West, most of them recorded in *Star of the West*. They can be your guides to making great speeches.

A very useful way to improve in this area is to join your local Toastmasters International Mens and Womens Club. This organization specializes in assisting people to overcome their fears and become better public speakers. For Bahá'ís, it can also be an excellent place to meet new people and speak on a wide variety of Bahá'í-related subjects.

## Direct Teaching

Direct teaching is a different way of finding the waiting souls. We go out directly to the masses instead of them coming to us. In fact, this has been tried in various shapes and stages all over the world for many decades. If properly done, you can reach souls in public places and their homes. These are people you have not met before. After conveying the Bahá'í message, you can invite them to join the religion of God for this day. This method has been successful in many places and it will increasingly be used to reach billions.

In connection to direct teaching there are two sub-categories: mass and door-to-door teaching. The following is a brief description of both to give you a taste of their nature, with enough information to decide whether to participate or not.

## Mass Teaching

It is done on a big scale. Usually it is organized by an institution such as a National or Local Spiritual Assembly or Teaching Committee. Hundreds of teachers participate, with elaborate planning and training.

Some of these projects can last from a few weeks to years. Mass teaching brings people to the Faith on a massive scale and participating can be one of the most rewarding experiences of a Bahá'í life. Such projects are happening all around the world at the same time. In your country, contact the Bahá'í National Center. If you want to participate elsewhere, get in touch with the Bahá'í World Center, Post Office Box 155, 31001, Haifa, Israel. The e-mail is **secretariat@bwc.com**.

## *Door-to-door Teaching*

In this method, the teacher goes from door to door in a neighborhood. The purpose can differ from place to place. For example, in some Caribbean countries, after work hours some pioneers go from house to house. They get to know the neighbors and if opportunity arises, to share the Faith. In some other countries, Bahá'ís go to every house in an area to announce an event.

When going to someone's home, one has to be careful. There is always a risk of offending someone. One should use extreme care and wisdom. The Universal House of Justice points out that:

> ...no teaching activity should be an encroachment on people's privacy, nor should it force the teachings upon unwilling listeners.
> (**Motlagh, Hushidar**, *Teaching: The Crown of Immortal Glory*, p. 297)

Also, one should be mindful of a directive from Shoghi Effendi regarding distribution of literature door-to-door.

> He feels that to distribute Bahá'í pamphlets from door-to-door...is undignified and might create a bad impression of the Faith. No doubt, it is eagerness and devotion of the friends that led them to make this proposal, but he does not think that the best interests of the Cause are served by such a method.
> (**Shoghi Effendi**, *A letter on his behalf*, dated Oct. 20, 1956)

# Word Check

| encroachment | advance beyond the original or proper limits. |
|---|---|
| impression | an effect produced on the mind. |
| eagerness | strong desire, enthusiasm. |

Some of us may be ambivalent about door-to-door teaching. Some like it and others don't. Its appropriateness differs from one country to another. In some countries, walking up to someone's home uninvited is not considered unusual—strangers are always welcomed. In other places, unexpected guests are not encouraged. In some cases, teaching door-to-door might give the impression of the Faith being a pushy religion. This method is one of the many ways to teach the Faith and you should choose whatever you feel comfortable doing. It is also essential to consult with the institutions of the Faith in each local area. They are in the best position to know which methods are best suited.

# TEACHING MOMENT—STUNNED AND OVERJOYED

The Universal House of Justice declared the year 1970 as "Operation Badi," in honor of the young Persian boy who sacrificed his life to deliver a message from Bahá'u'lláh to the Shah of Iran. A young man by the name of Gordon Kidd was a neighbor and friend of Dorothy Wingett and he became interested in the Faith. After some learning about the Faith, he lived with us. Although he was not a

Bahá'í yet, he asked if he could have a meeting in our home with just the youth, not with adults, so that they could discuss their problems with no fear of rejection or criticism. He also asked if we could invite some Bahá'í youth to talk to him and several of his friends.

Many youths from Oshawa came—included in this group were Al Moore, Walter Knox, and Doug Sawden. Also Dave Maunders and his pregnant wife arrived on a motorcycle. At the first meeting, Gord arrived with seven of his friends, and standing at the door, he apologized that he could not find more. We were stunned, overjoyed, and grateful for any to come.

This was the beginning of a series of Thursday night firesides where there were usually from 10 to 30 youth attending. The walls of our basement, on which they had drawn all the symbols of each Faith, literally bounced during the meetings. They would play their guitars and sing Bahá'í songs and share problems with one another.

Gordon Kidd eventually became a Bahá'í along with Mike and Brenda O'Toole, Dave Bucknell, Linda Miller, Janet Elmhirst, Rick Elliot, and Bob LaCourse. There are just too many to mention. These new Bahá'í youth were invited to give a talk at the United Church and, in turn, the young members of the church to attend a fireside. Seven of these church members eventually became Bahá'ís.

The new Bahá'ís carried their prayer books in their shirt pockets everywhere they went and the prayer books were very much in sight. During the summer of 1970, there were firesides going on all over the town both in homes and outdoor parks and there were over 90 young people who declared as a result of their intensive teaching efforts. A few of these even pioneered overseas and some on the homefront as well.

In Lakefield, a small town, there were a lot of rumors being spread that the Wingetts were selling drugs to these dozens of young people who were always hanging around both of the Wingett homes. The police cruised around these two houses on a daily basis. Although it was embarrassing, we did not mind. However, they never did come into the houses to check.

Linda Miller's mother, Norma, was so impressed with the changed behavior of her daughter that she invited the Bahá'ís to speak at a meeting to a group she belonged to called the "Seekers." Norma eventually declared too.

**Maddie Wingett**, Peterborough, Ontario, Canada

## Traveling Teaching

The Báb, after announcing the Letters of Living, immediately requested many of them to travel and proclaim His newly born religion. Some went to towns, villages, and cities of Iran. One even came from India looking for the Báb, and he was sent back to his native land.

Bahá'u'lláh, during His time on earth, encouraged many believers to travel far and near to make the Great Announcement. Many notable teachers traveled in Iran, India, Turkey, Iraq, and Egypt.

When 'Abdu'l-Bahá became the Head of the Bahá'í world, He too encouraged traveling teaching so that the message of His Prophet-Father could reach more countries, with focus on Western Europe and North America. When pilgrims went to the Holy Land, Haifa, Israel, to see Him, very lovingly He asked many to spend some time in Paris, London, and other European cities to offer others the glad tidings. Some of the notable teachers were May Bolles (Maxwell), Stanwood Cobb and Lua Getsinger. Finally when He was a free man, His own desire to be a traveling teacher was fulfilled. 'Abdu'l-Bahá, at the advanced age of 67, made an historical trip to Europe and North America, spending almost two and a half years. He proclaimed His Father's religion at churches, universities, public places, and in homes as an exemplary teacher.

When Shoghi Effendi became Guardian, the objective was to make the Bahá'í

Faith known to the whole world. Like the Central Figures, he encouraged traveling teaching as a major part of the expansion goal. Believers from many parts of the  world rose to the Guardian's challenge to travel.

*What is traveling teaching?* It simply means a Bahá'í goes to another town, city, country, or continent to share the message of Bahá'u'lláh. It has been part of the Bahá'í culture, a key part of its expansion process since the beginning of its birth. Nowadays, the Universal House of Justice, in its planning, determines where international teachers are needed and then assigns the responsibility of  supplying those teachers to various countries. National and local requirements are planned by National and Local Spiritual Assemblies.

## What are the Benefits of Traveling Teaching?

The benefits that we have seen regarding teaching also apply to traveling teaching. In addition to reaping divine rewards for imparting the life-giving Message, this is one of the greatest ways to appreciate our worldwide Bahá'í family. It gives a real sense of being part of building a new order on a global scale and, of course, we meet other Bahá'ís.

For traveling teachers, hospitality is often available. As the people of Bahá, offering hospitality to our fellow Bahá'ís is our privilege and duty. To find out what accommodation is available when teaching internationally, you may want to approach the appropriate agency at your National Bahá'í Center.

Hospitality is not always available and in such a case, the traveling teacher has to make his or her own  arrangements. Working together for the Faith this way is a great opportunity to build friendship and fellowship, visit far places, and experience other cultures, all of which can make the traveling teacher a better world citizen.

## *Preparing for Traveling Teaching*

If you are thinking of traveling teaching, you may want to consider the following tips:

- First, pick a place—far or near. It is a great way to spend your vacation. If you like warm places, go to Florida, California, the Caribbean Islands, Australia, India, Ecuador, Zanzibar, South Africa, Seychelles, Mauritius, or many other places around the world. Cooler places can be found in northern Canada, Greenland, Iceland, Norway and Sweden. (It is not always cold in these places. They sometimes enjoy very nice warm weather. And often the people have warm hearts.) In most places, there are Bahá'ís.
- Through the national institutions of your country, get in touch with the Bahá'ís in the target place and inform them of your plan.
- Consult on accommodation. Ask for suggestions about places to stay where you plan to teach. Discuss your needs, for example, for hospitality or to rent a room. Countries around the world have different standards; don't hesitate to ask about food, clothing, and sanitation. You want to make sure it will be a pleasant experience and not a terrible cultural shock. In traveling teaching there are always some tests and do not over-extend yourself at the expense of enjoying the experience. The places you stay can make or break your trip.
- Let them know the number of persons in your party. Don't hesitate to plan a teaching trip with your family. There are many advantages, and one of them is to serve Bahá'u'lláh as a family unit.
- Plan your itinerary, how to get there and back.
- Consult the Bahá'í institutions of the target place on what needs to be done and draw up a plan. Try to eliminate surprises. You will experience many of them anyway—hopefully pleasant ones.
- If you know ahead of time what the host community wants you to do, spend some time preparing talks, firesides, materials, videos, etc.
- Make sure you have appropriate attire.
- Plan for food, in case you need a special diet. Research the food of the place you are going to, and decide whether it meets your needs. Food can be another source of inconvenience and with some advance planning, you can

avoid difficulties.

- Pray for the success of your trip.
- Ask others to pray for you.
- Get there and have good teaching moments.
- Go home and tell your Bahá'í friends about your trip. Make sure they are envious of your trip. It is OK to do this in the teaching arena.

## Pioneering

So far, we have seen several kinds of teaching methods practiced in the Bahá'í world; the prince of all is pioneering, according to Bahá'u'lláh:

> Such a service is, indeed, the prince of all goodly deeds.
>
> (**Bahá'u'lláh**, *Gleanings from the Writings of Bahá'u'lláh*, p. 334)

Shoghi Effendi sets the priority through the statement below:

> The Guardian has pointed out that the most important service anyone can render the Faith today is to teach the Cause of God. The degree of importance of areas of service is first, pioneering in a virgin area of the Crusade, second, pioneering in one of the consolidation areas abroad, and third, settling in one of the goal cities of the homefront; and finally, teaching with redoubled effort wherever a Bahá'í may reside.
>
> (**Shoghi Effendi**, from a letter written on his behalf to an individual believer, August 22, 1954: *Lights of Guidance* pp. 439-440)

## What is Pioneering?

Pioneering simply means to move to another place to serve the Bahá'í Faith. There are two categories: overseas and homefront. Goal areas are determined by the Universal House of Justice, National Spiritual Assemblies, and sometimes by regional and local institutions.

Homefront pioneers are those who move within their country; overseas pioneers are those that leave their own country for another. Goal areas are determined during the current Bahá'í plan and a list can be obtained from the National Bahá'í Center or Bahá'í World Center.

Unlike traveling teachers, a pioneer of the Faith moves to a new place for a long period of time, for example from six months to a lifetime. Bahá'í pioneers work very hard to establish the Faith in virgin territories. They explore new areas of service much like pioneers in space, medicine, and education. Bahá'í pioneers are not only involved in teaching the Faith, but in transforming their new society. They serve in administration, education, and consolidation. Many get work to financially support themselves and also work in many Bahá'í social and economic programs.

The Bahá'í Faith has a long heroic history of pioneers who were like front-line soldiers. They moved to all corners of the world to spiritually conquer the planet Earth. The need for pioneers will continue to exist as we build the foundation of the Bahá'í World Order envisioned by Bahá'u'lláh and 'Abdu'l-Bahá.

Pioneers are encouraged to become part of the local community by making it their new home.

## Benefits of Pioneering

There are numerous advantages to pioneering. To hear inspiring stories, talk to a returned pioneer in your area. They will be delighted to explain the joy as well as the challenges of promoting the Faith in this way. Some are:

- The satisfaction of serving Bahá'u'lláh.
- All the graces of God are conferred upon a teacher.
- You receive from and give love to humanity.
- Spiritual growth.
- Opportunities to participate in many capacities.
- Experience of another culture.
- Your horizon of the world will be broadened.
- You will be challenged to develop complete reliance on Bahá'u'lláh.

 TEACHING MOMENT—A FULL CIRCLE

In Chester, England in 1965 I was a student nurse working my way towards my State Registered Nursing Diploma. While working on the men's surgical ward I met a young man from Iran who was a nursing assistant. Although in the beginning Shahi made comments about the cleanliness of nurses that caused some friction between us, Shahi and his friend Fari eventually invited me and a friend for coffee.

This initial friendship was followed by an invitation to a meeting at someone's home. My girlfriend declined to go but for some unknown reason I went. I really do not remember much about those meetings. I remember the house being small, cold, and draughty and people coming together who somehow seemed strangely out of place in those surroundings. I don't remember what was read and said. After a period of time, I moved to another hospital and they used to send an older gentleman to drive me to the meetings. I wasn't very comfortable traveling at night with a strange man in a car, and as a policeman's daughter, I was definitely questioning their motives. Later I was given a copy of the books, *Hidden Words* and *Prescription for Living. Hidden Words* had an impact on me because a fortune teller several years before had told me that someone would give me a book and that book would be everything to me. On an unconscious level I knew that *Hidden*

*Words* was that book but I still cannot explain why I knew that.

In 1967 I married and moved to Canada, bringing the two books with me. I mentioned the Bahá'í Faith to my husband, David, who thought from my description that it was an isolated group of people with their own beliefs. I never really thought about the Bahá'í Faith again for several years.

In January 1970, we went on holiday to Jamaica, and on our last day decided to take a bus tour of the island. During the journey someone in the back of the bus asked about the different religions on the island and questioned whether the guide knew of the Bahá'í Faith. In the front seat I was frantically nudging my husband and reminding him of the books at home. When we stopped for tea, I spoke to the lady and she showed me a ring on her finger that at the time held no meaning for me at all, and later became known to me as the ring symbol.

The following day we were to return to Canada but on the tour bus back to the hotel, a note was passed inviting us to visit the lady that evening.

That night we took a taxi to the home of Mr. and Mrs. Hadden. We also met Edyth MacArthur, Knight of Bahá'u'lláh, who asked the question on the bus. They spoke about Bahá'u'lláh and Mrs. Hadden generously gave us her copy of *Bahá'í World Faith*. They provided us with the phone numbers of Bahá'ís in our area and encouraged us to continue our search for truth.

On our return home to Canada, we contacted Doug and Ann Wilson in King City, Ontario, and through them we met Dick and Eleanor Harding. Between January and April, we attended many meetings and read everything we could possibly get our hands on. In April after a fireside at which Anwar Hanna spoke at the Harding home, the Bahá'ís were talking about attending a National Convention in Toronto the following week, and we expressed a desire to attend. We were advised that the meeting was for Bahá'ís only so we asked how we could become Bahá'ís. Having signed the cards and with a letter confirming our recent declaration, we attended the Convention, and there sitting behind us was my friend Shahi, my very first contact with the Bahá'í Faith. I felt that I had come full circle.

We later learned that Edyth MacArthur had tried to pioneer to Jamaica but was unsuccessful in finding work or being able to stay. Edyth told us that she never felt her trip had been for nothing as she was obviously meant to be there.

**Vicky Hill,** Sharon, Ontario, Canada

# Examples

With teaching, opportunities knock at unexpected moments. How many times have you had a listener, but were not prepared to say anything? Afterwards, you felt bad about missing a good chance. Ideally, you want to be connected to the Holy Spirit during your teaching moments. Though everyone experiences "downtime" once in a while, you want some handy tools in your tool belt to reach for when you need help.

Some of those teaching tools are scripts of different lengths, say one, two or five minutes. You can prepare your presentation according to your own taste. The following is an example that is an answer to the question "What is the Bahá'í Faith?". It is approximately three minutes long.

## What is the Bahá'í Faith?

The Bahá'í Faith is an independent world religion. It was started in 1844 in Iran by the Prophet-Forerunner The Báb, and later firmly established by Bahá'u'lláh. Since then, it has been established in about 230 countries.

Bahá'ís consider Bahá'u'lláh to be the Messenger of God for this day. He wrote over a hundred volumes on numerous spiritual and social subjects and His work has been translated into 802 languages. Bahá'u'lláh's main teachings are the *oneness of God*, the *oneness of religion*, and the *oneness of mankind*.

The oneness of God simply means that there is one God who is the Creator of the whole universe. He created humans in His own image and likeness and our purpose in life is to know and love Him. God makes Himself known to us through His Prophets.

This brings us to the second principle: the oneness of religion. Bahá'u'lláh teaches that the Founders of all the major world religions, including Abraham, Krishna, Moses, Zoroaster, Buddha, Jesus Christ, and Muhammad, are Messengers from God. Their spiritual teachings are the same, but their social teachings differ according to the critical needs of the age each Messenger lived on earth. Referring to these religions, Bahá'u'lláh said:

```
These principles and laws, these firmly
established and mighty systems, have proceeded
from one Source, and are the rays of one Light.
```
   **(Bahá'u'lláh**, *Gleanings from the Writings of Bahá'u'lláh*, pp. 287-288)

The oneness of mankind means that human beings are all created as noble spiritual souls. The diversity we see among us is to be appreciated rather than eliminated. The Bahá'í world community is made up of about 2100 ethnic, racial and tribal groups scattered around the whole world.

About the human family Bahá'u'lláh said:

```
Ye are the fruit of one tree, and the leaves of
one branch...The earth is but one country, and
mankind its citizens.
```
   **(Bahá'u'lláh**, *Gleanings from the Writings of Bahá'u'lláh*, p. 250)

The Bahá'í Faith offers a very bright future for humanity with tremendous excitement and optimism. Bahá'u'lláh has promised the Most Great Peace will be established on earth.

TEACHING MOMENT—MY QUESTION

TO GOD

It occurred about 30 years ago, when I was young. I am from a Muslim background, particularly the Sunni sect. The society in which I was living was split (and still is) by numerous thoughts; one which my family belonged to was obviously the right one, but all these sects saddened me very much. I hoped to see a united Muslim society, so I made many moves to unite it, but I was not successful.

So life continued as it was and in 1959, I got married and a difficult period began for me and my wife which lasted for six years approximately, during which we encountered the loss of two sons. Illnesses affected others and my wife too was affected by illness.

In this darkest period, I used to meditate upon my fate and to make my mea-culpa, thinking that because I am not a good Muslim that is why these things are happening to me and my family. According to Muslim law, one who doesn't say prayers or fast, as stated in the Qur'án, is doomed to hell on the day of the last judgment. So I was consigned to hell and this made me sad. But one thing made me happy, and that was—on that day of Judgment when God would order me to hell—l would put a question to Him: "whether He sent a prophet for me?" By this question God was challenged and I was happy, my mind was at peace and all my troubles were forgotten. This state of things continued till one day while reading the newspaper, I came across the word "Bahá'ís." They were holding their convention and this occupied my mind for a while, thinking that it may be a club or other such organization.

Time passed on and much later, while returning home with my wife and sick child from the hospital where I had gone for X-rays, I spotted a sign on a building in Port Louis, Mauritius, that said, "Bahá'í Center." I stopped for a moment and wanted to inquire, but I didn't because the child was suffering, so I made my way home. But the word Bahá'í troubled me very much.

I had a friend (and he still is) named Swalleh Eradhun; he was a nursing officer and was working as such at the clinic of the village. We seldom met and I used to inquire about him from another friend, Aman Muddhoo, who owned a shop in the same village. Whenever I came from my work I used to go to the shop to buy cigarettes and thus to chat with him and inquire about Swalleh. One day a man sitting inside the shop—Hamid Muddhoo (whose son is a Bahá'í now)—rose up and told me "don't you know Swalleh has become a Bahá'í?" It was the third time that the word Bahá'í struck me, and this time I had the opportunity to inquire, so I asked "what is a Bahá'í?" He told it was a religion. "Who is the founder?" The reply came: "Bahá'u'lláh."

On hearing the name "Bahá'u'lláh," I was thrilled from the bottom to the top of my being; time stopped for a while; I spoke no more. I made up my mind to find the whereabouts of Swalleh and to know more about Bahá'í. Six months later I accepted the Faith of Bahá'u'lláh. I was made a new creation, I was very happy, my life and that of my family took a new turn. Then I came to realize that I didn't challenge God with my question but rather He answered it by letting me know about Bahá'u'lláh and His teaching.

Adversities came across from the Muslim society but I met them with happiness in the name of Bahá'u'lláh. My wife followed in my footsteps after three years and accepted the faith. She supported me and Swalleh to propagate the Faith in Brisée-Verdière, Mauritius, and its surroundings.

Today, by the Grace of God, all my children are Bahá'ís on their own terms and I pray Him that I may end my life on this earth as a Bahá'í.

**Nizam Lagan**, Brisée Verdière, Mauritius

## Summary

The secret of delivering Bahá'u'lláh's message effectively is two fold. First, one must become a channel between the Holy Spirit and the seeking soul. It is a method used by 'Abdu'l-Bahá, the Apostles of Christ and all the great spiritual teachers in the past. This connection allows you to become a 'hollow reed' through which the right words in the most appropriate dosage flow from the Source of all knowledge to the seeker. Therefore, you let the Holy Spirit do the talking.

Second, the agent that unclogs the impurities of this channel is the divine qualities acquired by the teacher, through spiritual practices such as prayer, fasting, meditation, study of the Writings, service and improving of character.

In the Bahá'í world we have developed many methods of delivering the message, such as pioneering, traveling teaching, and firesides. There are no hard and fast rules about them. You can choose the method you are comfortable with. And there is always room for new approaches.

# TEACHING BREAK

A sense of humour is good... to a point

# 6

## Understanding Entry by Troops

Entry by troops is simply a milestone in the development of the Bahá'í Faith. We have seen many milestones in the past and this one is to happen in the near future. Recently it is often mentioned in messages from the Universal House of Justice and in local teaching plans. Entry by troops is supposed to be a big step forward. Before this major event happens, there are many things that have to take place first. Its very existence depends on other events. Entry by troops is the end result.

It is like a farmer who envisions an abundant crop at the end of a season. At the beginning of the growing season, he is very well aware of many tasks that are ahead of him. Between an empty field and a harvest there are many steps that he has to take before a fruitful growing season happens. In his mind, he goes through some of the steps: till the soil, plant the seeds, irrigate the land, fertilize the plants, discourage the insects, and protect the crop. He can only expect a good result if he takes all the necessary steps at the right time.

Entry by troops, we will soon find out, is very much like the harvesting of the crop—it is not an independent event, rather, its occurrence is only going to take place if the right conditions are achieved by the Bahá'ís. It is tied to many preceding events; otherwise, it will not happen.

Understanding the dependencies of both the individuals and institutions is crucial to the success of entry by troops. In the following pages we will see extracts related to entry by troops from letters of the Guardian and the Universal House of Justice, copied from *Teaching the Bahá'í Faith*, compiled by the Research Department of the Universal House of Justice. They explain the conditions that will allow entry by troops to flourish.

# Prophecy

*Where does the idea of entry by troops originate?*  According to a memorandum from The Research Department of the Universal House of Justice, dated May 4, 1993, that souls will join the Bahá'í Faith in great numbers has been alluded to in the Qur'án 110:2 which states: "And thou seest men entering the religion of God by troops."  And Bahá'u'lláh and 'Abdu'l-Bahá both have made reference to this prediction at numerous times.

In the following passage, the Guardian elaborated on this prophecy. He said:

> Such a **steady flow of reinforcements** is absolutely vital and is of extreme urgency, for nothing short of the vitalizing influx of new blood that will reanimate the world Bahá'í Community can safeguard the prizes which, at so great a sacrifice, involving the expenditure of so much time, effort and treasure, are now being won in virgin territories by Bahá'u'lláh's valiant Knights.
>
> This flow, moreover, will presage and hasten the advent of the day which, as prophesied by 'Abdu'l-Bahá, will witness the **entry by troops** of peoples of divers nations and races into the Bahá'í world—a day which, viewed in its proper perspective, will be the prelude to that long-awaited hour when a **mass conversion** on the part of these same nations and races, and as a direct result of a chain of

events, momentous and possibly catastrophic in nature... will suddenly revolutionize the fortunes of the Faith, derange the equilibrium of the world, and reinforce a thousandfold the numeric strength as well as the material power and the spiritual authority of the Faith of Bahá'u'lláh.

(**Shoghi Effendi**, *Citadel of Faith: Messages to America 1947-1957*, pp. 116-117)

 # Word Check

| valiant | brave, courageous. |
|---------|--------------------|
| presage | to foreshadow. |

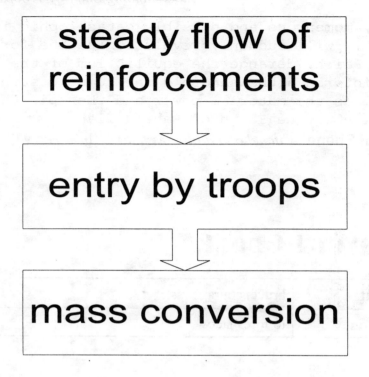

steady flow of reinforcements

entry by troops

mass conversion

# TEACHING MOMENT—PURITY OF

# HEART AND LOVE

This was 1988 in Belize, around February. There had been a teaching project, it was in its first year in Belize, by the NSA. And it had four full-time teachers, one Belizean and three pioneers. These folks had continued full-time teaching one whole year and they were really exhausted. And four Canadians from Saskatchewan came down to join the project and these teachers were so happy to see us and so relieved, that they all just kind of collapsed and went back to their families and homes and recuperated and rested. And then we picked up the reins for about a month or month and a half, we filled their spots. And they had really done the prayers and the initial work and they had already designated some areas. And in this one area, this small community, the word "tyranny" wouldn't be too strong for explaining the influence of a group of youth that they had. There was a band of about twenty youth lived in this small trench town that really frightened and intimidated the community. And they would steal things and they would harass the girls if it was at night. And they hung out and did drugs and stuff and the community was quite fearful. And one of the things that happened is we taught all of these young people. All of these young men became Bahá'ís. And it was kind of an exciting story in itself. But I am only using that as a prelude to say that and this was not a teaching story that was without tests and problems, because these young men had a pretty difficult life style. And they made some significant changes in it, but it wasn't entirely that easy for the Bahá'í community and for them. But this affected deeply the community they lived in. And the community took note of the Bahá'í Faith, because the community where these boys were from thought, if these boys can be reached and they can be changed, this is something powerful. And we really noticed a receptivity. Once these young people became Bahá'ís, that whole village, there was a real, a kind of an upsurgence of hope and faith and an eagerness to listen and a receptivity towards the Bahá'í Faith.

And just to give you a sense of the expectancy, we would go from street to street, from house to house, door to door, asking people if they'd heard about the Faith and if they were interested. And in underdeveloped countries like this, this is a very commonplace way of approaching people and people invite you into their home and serve you tea. And it's not a question of they're going to instantly follow your religion, it's more out of politeness and courtesy and curiosity and a certain respect for any religion. So in this one instance, I recall we came down the street, to kind of describe this to you a little bit, it's muddy, there's a trench across the path, you have to walk across a little rickety bridge, very poor. I knocked at the door and someone answered. There was a couple of us. I said, 'would you like to hear about the Bahá'í Faith?' And they said, 'Oh, yes. We would very much like to hear about the Bahá'í Faith. We've been waiting for you.' And we entered the room and all of the people were dressed up in their best clothes. And it was as if they had been sitting waiting just for us. We came in and one of the children was a retarded child. This child was like pure spirit. Really it was like walking into a room and a light bulb was shining through this child's face. The family obviously was very religious and very reverent. They said we know you have a message, because we had a dream, I'm not sure if it was the husband or the wife. They had a dream the night before, or just a couple of nights before. And in the dream they saw Christ. And they said He was dressed like a bridegroom, but He was wearing jeans. And they said He told them to look out, because He was coming again and He had a message for them and they were to watch and listen for when He came so they would recognize this message. And they said, when you came and you were wearing jeans and you said you had a message from God, we knew that it was important and we were waiting. And this whole family, I just said the name 'Bahá'í' and a few things, they said, 'yes, we accept, we believe'. They said we want to know things about the religion, but we accept it, we believe it, they didn't have to be taught. And it was such a confirmation. And the love in that family was surprising. We felt, in a sense, like beggars at a banquet, because of their purity of heart and love.

**Ted Glabush**, Calgary, Alberta, Canada

# Definition

Definition is important. One that is clear and precise helps us understand better what we are trying to define. And a good definition also guards us from taking the wrong action, if anything needs to be done. For example, if you explain to a one-year-old baby how to buy a loaf of bread at the store, she will not understand it and there is no chance that she will be able to execute this task. However, if you do the same thing to a twelve-year-old, she will comprehend the idea as well as be able to do the task, even the first time.

Now let's look at understanding and action in a different way; one is able to comprehend an idea but the understanding may be incorrect. The classic case of misunderstanding and unexpected results is the voyage of Christopher Columbus. In 1492, this experienced navigator set sail from a port in Spain to find a westward route to Asia by sea. Due to a misunderstanding of the ocean and land masses, he landed on an island near the south east coast of Florida, USA, very far from Asia.

In the previous quotation, we saw three successive processes: steady flow of reinforcements, entry by troops, and mass conversion. Before we continue, let's look at what they mean. If we take a community or region of the world, these three phrases suggest the Bahá'í population of that location will grow at these three distinct paces, one following at a greater rate than the previous one.

The following passages give more detail in terms of rate of growth:

In response to your letter... in which you seek clarification of the terms "troops" and "masses" as used by the beloved Guardian in the celebrated passage to which you refer, the Universal House of Justice directs us to say that the specific definitions that you are seeking are not found in the Writings. It is obvious, as you imply, that the stage of "entry by troops" is a prelude to "mass conversion."

**(The Universal House of Justice**, *a letter written on its behalf to an individual believer dated 23 February 1988*)

The concept of mass teaching may be better understood if put in the context of "teaching the masses." This implies reaching every level of society in every continent and island in the world.

**(The Universal House of Justice**, *a letter written on its behalf to an individual believer dated 11 August 1988*)

When the masses of mankind are awakened and enter the Faith of God, a new process is set in motion and the growth of a new civilization begins. Witness the emergence of Christianity and of Islam. These masses are the rank and file, steeped in traditions of their own, but receptive to the new

Word of God, by which, when they truly respond to
it, they become so influenced as to transform those
who come in contact with them.

**(The Universal House of Justice**, *a letter to all National Spiritual
Assemblies dated 13 July 1964, published in Wellspring of Guidance:
Messages 1963-1968, pp. 31-33*)

---

**Warning!!!!**

Some duplications have purposely been
included in the following sections. Proceed
with tolerance.

---

# Growth Does Not Mean Progress

In time you will see how abundant the fruit of your
services will be. It is not sufficient to number the
souls that embrace the Cause to know the progress
that it is making. The more important consequences of
your activities are the spirit that is diffused into
the life of the community, and the extent to which
the teachings we proclaim  become part of the
consciousness and belief of the people that hear
them. For it is **only when the spirit has thoroughly
permeated the world** that the people will begin to
enter the Faith in large numbers. At the beginning of
spring only the few, exceptionally favored seeds will
sprout, but when the season gets in its full sway,
and the atmosphere gets permeated with the warmth of
the true springtime, the masses of flowers will begin
to appear, and a whole hillside suddenly blooms. We
are still in the state when only isolated souls are
awakened, but soon we shall have the full swing of

the season and the quickening of whole groups and
nations into the spiritual life breathed by
Bahá'u'lláh.

(**Shoghi Effendi**, *a letter written on his behalf to an individual dated 18
February 1932*)

# Promote Love and Unity

Too great emphasis cannot be laid on the importance
of the **unity** of the friends, for only by manifesting
the greatness of their **love** for and patience with
each other can they hope to attract large numbers to
their ranks.

(**Shoghi Effendi**, *a letter written on his behalf to an individual dated 2
August 1942*)

He longs to see a greater degree of **unity and love**
among the believers, for these are the spirit which
must animate their community life. Until the people
of the world see a shining example set by us they
will not embrace the Cause in masses, because they
require to see the teachings demonstrated in a
pattern of action.

(**Shoghi Effendi**, *a letter written on his behalf to a Bahá'í Winter School
session dated 13 March 1944*)

Dear Mr. and Mrs. ... **have a great ability for
kindling in the hearts the love of God.** It is for
this wholesome, warming, spiritualizing love that the
world is thirsting today. The Bahá'ís will never
succeed in attracting large numbers to the Faith
until they see in our individual and community life

acts, and the atmosphere, that bespeaks the love of God.

(**Shoghi Effendi**, *a letter written on his behalf to an individual dated 17 February 1945*)

Without the **spirit of real love for Bahá'u'lláh, for His Faith and its Institutions, and the believers for each other**, the Cause can never really bring in large numbers of people. For it is not preaching and rules the world wants, but love and action.

(**Shoghi Effendi**, *a letter written on his behalf to an individual dated 25 October 1949*)

 Word Check

| permeate | to pass or flow or spread into every part of. |
| --- | --- |
| sway | swing. |
| bespeak | to indicate, to be evidence of. |

 TEACHING MOMENT—LUCKY ME!

I had a beauty salon in the small town of Lakefield, Ontario, Canada. One day in late September 1960, a lady named Gladys Tranter (now deceased and the most spirited Bahá'í I have ever met) came into my shop to have her hair done. She mentioned the Indian people on the Curve Lake Reservation, not far from Lakefield. Then she began to talk about the oneness of humanity. I asked if she was a Jehovah's Witness as they are always preaching. She said, "No, I am a Bahá'í." Of course, I said, "A what?" It took me a few days to even say the name right.

The next time Gladys was in the shop, she told me that Christ had returned. The hair on the back of my neck stood straight up. I wanted to meet Him. I had always wondered if He would ever return. I was raised a Catholic but could not accept most of the teachings. For a while I was a Baptist. All they talked about was the return of Christ. Of course, I was stunned as I never thought it would happen in my life time and if He did return surely everyone would know about Him.

Well, she told me more about the principles, which I found very attractive. Bahá'u'lláh being the return of Christ was an added bonus. I told her that Bahá'í Faith sounded more like a way of life, rather than a religion. Religion to me was attending church every Sunday and forgetting about it for the rest of the week. She replied, "Well, religion is a way of life."

I wondered why I didn't learn about this wonderful news at school. Soon, I found out that only Bahá'ís believed in this. I became so excited that I could hardly continue working on her hair. Gladys had extremely fine and delicate hair, requiring a lot of extra attention. By mistake, I frizzed her hair. Now, today, frizzed hair is a desired hairdo, which costs a fortune. But in those days, I could get fired for it. So it took me a long time to correct the mess.

She always said that I was the ripest plum she had ever picked and it was all for a worthy cause. I can understand a little of how the early believers could utterly leave themselves when they hear about the Faith and not know where they are or what happens to their hair.

I went to several firesides at the Gladys and Richard Tranter home in Woodview, twenty miles north of Lakefield. Richard, her husband was also a Bahá'í. I had recently moved from the big city of Toronto; therefore, I was very nervous about the country roads, especially in the dark. I enticed a girlfriend of mine to go with me the first time as I was so frightened, but was so strongly attracted to the teachings of the Faith. Unfortunately, my friend never became a Bahá'í.

On New Year's Eve 1960, I was all set to join my pals for the usual celebration, when suddenly I had the overwhelming urge to visit Gladys and Richard. I always called Gladys the Bahá'í fanatic: you couldn't talk with her about any subject that she didn't link to a Bahá'í principle. She was devoted and knowledgeable. Lucky for me, they were home and available. We sat up the entire night playing cribbage and talked about the Faith. At dawn, on January 1, 1961, I declared my belief in Bahá'u'lláh.

It was the happiest moment of my life. I remember saying I would never be "free" until I became a Bahá'í, as it would haunt me for the rest of my life. In those days, before one became a Bahá'í, one had to first study the Will and Testament of 'Abdu'l-Bahá, then write to the National Spiritual Assembly stating the reasons for joining. All very scary and unusual to say the least. Then we had to meet with the National Teaching Committee.

**Maddie Wingett**, Peterborough, Ontario, Canada

# Spiritual Transformation

Although tremendous progress has been made in the United States during the last quarter of a century, he feels that the believers must ever-increasingly become aware of the fact that only to the degree that they **mirror forth in their joint lives the exalted standards of the Faith** will they attract the masses to the Cause of God.

(**Shoghi Effendi**, *a letter written on his behalf to a Bahá'í school session dated 15 September 1951*)

When the true spirit of teaching, which calls for

**complete dedication, consecration to the noble mission**, and living the life, is fulfilled, not only by the individuals, but by the Assemblies also, then the Faith will grow by leaps and bounds.

    (**Shoghi Effendi**, a letter written on his behalf to a Local Spiritual Assembly dated 19 March 1954)

The Bahá'ís will never succeed in attracting large numbers to the Faith until they see in our individual and community life acts, and the atmosphere, that bespeaks the love of God.

    (**Shoghi Effendi**, *a letter written on his behalf to an individual dated 17 February 1945*)

 Word Check

| dedication | 1. to devote to a sacred person or use. <br> 2. to devote one's time and energy to a special purpose. |
|---|---|
| consecration | 1. to make or declare sacred. <br> 2. to dedicate formally to the service or worship of God. |

# An Alternative Life Style

Until **the public sees in the Bahá'í Community a true pattern**, in action, of something better than it already has, it will not respond to the Faith in large numbers.

    (**Shoghi Effendi**, *a letter written on his behalf to a individual dated 13 March 1944*)

He longs to see a greater degree of unity and love among the believers, for these are the spirits which must **animate their Community life**. Until the **people of the world see a shining example** set by us they will not embrace the Cause in masses, because they require to see the teachings demonstrated in a pattern of action.

(**Shoghi Effendi**, *a letter written on his behalf to a Bahá'í Winter School session dated 13 March 1944*)

Although tremendous progress has been made in the United States during the last quarter of a century, he feels that the believers must ever-increasingly become aware of the fact that only to the degree that they mirror forth in their joint lives the exalted standards of the Faith will they attract the masses to the Cause of God.

(**Shoghi Effendi**, *a letter written on his behalf to a Bahá'í school session dated 15 September 1951*)

# Process of Social Decline

Must humanity, tormented as she now is, be afflicted with still severer tribulations ere their purifying influence can prepare her to enter the heavenly Kingdom destined to be established upon earth? Must the inauguration of so vast, so unique, so illumined an era in human history be ushered in by so great a catastrophe in human affairs as to recall, nay surpass, the appalling collapse of Roman civilization in the first centuries of the Christian era? Must a series of **profound convulsions stir and rock the human race** ere Bahá'u'lláh can be enthroned in the hearts and consciences of the masses, ere His undisputed ascendancy is universally recognized, and the noble edifice of His World Order is reared and established?

(**Shoghi Effendi**, *The World Order of Bahá'u'lláh: Selected Letters, pp. 201-202*)

There are two things which will contribute greatly to bringing more people into the Cause more swiftly: one is **the maturity of the Bahá'ís within their Communities, functioning according to Bahá'í laws and in the proper spirit of unity,** and the other is the disintegration of society and the suffering it will bring in its wake. When the old forms are seen to be hopelessly useless, the people will stir from their materialism and spiritual lethargy, and embrace the Faith.

(**Shoghi Effendi**, *a letter written on his behalf to a individual dated 3 July 1948*)

 Word Check

| | |
|---|---|
| **tribulation** | a great affliction. |
| **convulsion** | a violent upheaval. |
| **ascendancy** | the state of being dominant. |
| **edifice** | a large building. |
| **lethargy** | extreme lack of energy or vitality. |

# Elements of Growth

Teaching the Faith embraces many diverse activities, all of which are vital to success, and each of which reinforces the other...

The aim, therefore, of all Bahá'í institutions and Bahá'í teachers is **to advance continually to new areas and strata of society**, with such thoroughness that, as the spark of faith kindles the hearts of the hearers, the teaching of the believers continues until, and even after, they **shoulder their responsibilities as Bahá'ís and participate in both the teaching and administrative work of the Faith.**

There are now many areas in the world where thousands of people have accepted the Faith so quickly that it has been beyond the capacity of the existing communities to consolidate adequately these advances. The people in these areas must be progressively deepened in their understanding of the Faith, in accordance with well-laid plans, so that their communities may, as soon as possible, become sources of great strength to the work of the Faith and begin to manifest the pattern of Bahá'í life.

   (**The Universal House of Justice**, *a letter to all National Spiritual Assemblies dated 25 May 1975*)

The teaching work, both that organized by institutions of the Faith and that which is the fruit of individual initiative, must be actively carried forward so that there will be growing numbers of believers, leading more countries to the stage of entry by troops and ultimately to mass conversion.

   (**The Universal House of Justice**, *Naw-Rúz 1979 Message*)

The Faith of God does not advance at one uniform pace. Sometimes it is like the advance of the sea when the tide is rising. Meeting a sandbank the water seems to be held back, but, with a new wave, it surges forward, flooding past the barrier which checked it for a little while. If the friends will but persist in their efforts, the cumulative effect of years of work will suddenly appear.

(**The Universal House of Justice**, *a letter written to a National Spiritual Assembly dated 27 July 1980*)

## Time is Now

The confusion of the world is not diminishing, rather does it increase with each passing day, and **men and women are losing faith in human remedies**. Realization is at last dawning that "There is no place to flee to" save God. Now is the golden opportunity; people are willing, in many places eager, to listen to the divine remedy.

(**The Universal House of Justice**, *Ridván 1965 Message to the Bahá'ís of the World*)

 TEACHING MOMENT—THE SECRET OF LIFE

As far as I can remember, I was always keen in the religious belief and practices of my forebears and, later when I came to know, in the religions of neighbors and friends. I considered myself devout and proud of being a Hindu and always attended discourses on Hindu religion and read books about it. So much that I knew that I knew things. But the secret pride didn't last long. I got my big shock in my early twenties. My Muslim friends always got a better word in matters of religion. I could not beat them--their arguments were so practically good and right. Their arguments issued from a different matrix, and that was their stronghold. I didn't understand then—that their revelation was nearer to us in time and provided more actual resources for life.

My losing in the argument, I felt, was because of not knowing enough. Often, after these defeats, I would pore over books looking for stronger arguments to impress them and beat them. But still I came back defeated.

Their religion was so close to life, so practical, so useful--as if sacred knowledge had been brought to earth to serve life. These defeats bothered me for a long time.

Surely, I reasoned with myself, God should know that I was a vegetarian and a follower of Sanatan Dharma, and He should not allow me to be defeated.

One day, still in my early twenties, in the Bonanza Bookshop in Port Louis, I chanced upon a book. A greenish-gray old book *Paris Talks* by 'Abdu'l-Bahá. My intuition said, 'Read this book and you will defeat the Muslim friends.' I brought the book home. They were talks delivered by 'Abdu'l-Bahá in Paris in Persian and the book was an English rendering of those talks. Very plain talks with simple words. Simple English words, but I could not get the message of the book. A big challenge.

Time passed and other books were piled on top of that book on my bedside table. Shame! Some old memory flashed in during this period. One late uncle, Bhajun Takoorparsad, had spoken to me of the Bahá'ís, of their knowing all the secrets of life and had asked me to look out for them, and join them if I wished my early life to be of some good account. I remembered even writing to them at the Bahá'í Institute, Belle Rose, Mauritius. But they had not replied. Surely they chose their members, I had presumed, and gone bitter at the rejection. Then I had consoled myself that having gotten hold of one of their books, I would be able to pierce their veil and know their secrets. But alas--that book remained a mystery and, secretly, a shame for me. I, who boasted about Hardy, Dickens and Stevenson had become a fool before a book of talks. When you are baffled by something, your inner self takes up the task and continues the work to solve the mystery for you.

Eventually some years later, more than two but less than five, I met one Bahá'í, Mr. Garcon Ungamootoo, when he came to spread the message of the Faith in my village. Through him I met Mr. Afsin and Mrs. Kohli Bahram, both Bahá'ís from India. Through their explanation, I gathered they were building a new society—in this present society the individual should be golden. Mr. Afsin (his was the first talk on the Faith I ever listened to in the classroom style) spoke nearly above my head. I recall the highlights. The world order being rolled up and a new order being spread. Very eloquent. Very impressive. Very confident. He emphasized that the job of building the new world order was ours and the sooner we do it, the better. The most important task, God's plan for humanity for this age, has been confided through Bahá'u'lláh to His followers and that task is the building up of the new world order. In 1979 I became a Bahá'í.

I came back to my Muslim friends and presented them new arguments (backed by the Bahá'í Faith ). Now they were adamant. Since I told them that the Bahá'í Faith was a Revelation after the Qur'án they said that their religion is the best and their Prophet the Last One from God. I thought that my failing to persuade them was just a matter of not knowing better. So, being already conversant with them, now I pursued my task of knowing more--I decided if I could not beat them, at least, I could win their respect. All I needed was time and willingness to mature. At that time there was no point that any religiously bigoted friend could put forward to silence me. I would always see the flaw and point out a better idea or show them the drawbacks of keeping their opinion. Their not listening or their not understanding is a different matter. In my heart I am persuaded that I have a truth which they don't have.

**Mukesh Poonyth,** Rose-Hill, Mauritius

# Universal Participation

The second challenge facing us is to **raise the intensity of teaching to a pitch never before attained**, in order to realize that "vast increase" called for in the Plan. Universal participation and constant action will win this goal. Every believer has a part to play, and is capable of playing it, for every soul meets others, and, as promised by Bahá'u'lláh, "Whosoever ariseth to aid Our Cause God will render him victorious..."

   (**The Universal House of Justice**, *Ridván 1965 Message to the Bahá'ís of the World*)

Efforts to **reach the minorities** should be increased and broadened to include all minority groups such as the Indians, Spanish-speaking people, Japanese and Chinese. Indeed, every stratum of American society must be reached and can be reached with the healing Message, if the believers will but arise and go forth with the spirit which is conquering the citadels of the southern states. Such a programme, coupled as it must be with continuous consolidation, can be effectively carried out by **universal participation** on the part of every lover of Bahá'u'lláh.

   (**The Universal House of Justice**, *Messages from the Universal House of Justice, 1968-1973*, pp. 85-86)

# Expansion and Consolidation

**Expansion** and **consolidation** are twin processes that must go hand in hand. The friends must not stop expansion in the name of consolidation. **Deepening the**

**newly enrolled believers** generates tremendous stimulus which results in further expansion. The enrolment of new believers, on the other hand, creates a new spirit in the community and provides additional potential manpower that will reinforce the consolidation work.

(**The Universal House of Justice**, *Wellspring of Guidance: Messages 1963-1968*, pp. 31-33)

This teaching work must include prompt, thorough and continuing consolidation so that all victories will be safeguarded, the number of Local Spiritual Assemblies will be increased and the foundations of the Cause reinforced.

(**The Universal House of Justice**, *Naw-Rúz 1979 Message to the Bahá'ís of the World*)

While this vital teaching work is progressing each National Assembly must ever bear in mind that expansion and consolidation are inseparable processes that must go hand in hand... To ensure that the spiritual life of the individual believer is continuously enriched, that local communities are becoming increasingly conscious of their collective duties, and that the institutions of an evolving administration are operating efficiently, is, therefore, as important as expanding into new fields and bringing in the multitudes under the shadow of the Cause.

(**The Universal House of Justice**, *a letter to all National Spiritual Assemblies engaged in mass teaching work dated 2 February 1966*)

Consolidation is as vital a part of the teaching work as expansion. It is that aspect of teaching which assists the believers to **deepen their knowledge and**

**understanding of the Teachings**, and fans the flame of their devotion to Bahá'u'lláh and His Cause, so that they will, of their own volition, continue the process of their spiritual development, promote the teaching work, and **strengthen the functioning of their administrative institutions**. Proper consolidation is essential to the preservation of the spiritual health of the community, to the protection of its interests, to the upholding of its good name, and ultimately to the continuation of the work of expansion itself.

(**The Universal House of Justice**, *a letter on behalf of the Universal House of Justice to all National Spiritual Assemblies dated 17 April 1981*)

## A Model to the World

Whenever a Bahá'í community exists, whether large or small, let it be distinguished for its abiding sense of security and faith, its high standard of rectitude, its complete freedom from all forms of prejudice, the spirit of love among its members and for the closely knit fabric of its social life. The acute distinction between this and present day society will inevitably arouse the interest of the more enlightened, and as the world's gloom deepens the light of Bahá'í life will shine brighter and brighter until its brilliance must eventually attract the disillusioned masses and cause them to enter the haven of the Covenant of Bahá'u'lláh, Who alone can bring them peace and justice and an ordered life.

(**The Universal House of Justice**, *Messages from the Universal House of Justice, 1968-1973*, p. 12)

**Strengthening and development of Local Spiritual Assemblies** is a vital objective of the Five Year

Plan. Success in this one goal will **greatly enrich the quality of Bahá'í life**, will heighten the capacity of the Faith to deal with entry by troops which is even now taking place and, above all, will demonstrate the solidarity and ever-growing distinctiveness of the Bahá'í community, thereby attracting more and more thoughtful souls to the Faith and offering a refuge to the leaderless and hapless millions of the spiritually bankrupt, moribund present order.

(**The Universal House of Justice**, *Naw-Rúz 1974 Message to the Bahá'ís of the World*)

 Word Check

| rectitude | a moral goodness, correctness of behavior or procedure. |
| --- | --- |
| solidarity | unity resulting from common interests or feelings or sympathies. |
| hapless | unlucky. |
| moribund | in a dying state, no longer effective. |

# Reaching the People of Capacity

Thus far, we have achieved a marvellous diversity in the large numbers of ethnic groups represented in the Faith, and everything should be done to fortify it through larger enrolments from among groups already represented and the attraction of members from groups not yet reached. However, there is another category of diversity which must be built up and without which the Cause will not be able adequately to meet the challenges being thrust upon it. Its membership, regardless of ethnic variety, needs now to **embrace increasing numbers of people of capacity,** including persons of accomplishment and prominence in the various fields of human endeavour. Enrolling significant numbers of such persons is an indispensable aspect of teaching the masses, an aspect which cannot any longer be neglected and which must be consciously and deliberately incorporated into our teaching work, so as to broaden its base and accelerate the process of entry by troops. So important and timely is the need for action on this matter that we are impelled to call upon Continental Counsellors and National Spiritual Assemblies to devote serious attention to it in their consultations and plans.

**(The Universal House of Justice,** *Ridván 1990 Message to the Bahá'ís of the World*)

 **Word Check**

| fortify | 1. to strengthen (a place) against attack, especially by constructing fortifications.<br>2. to strengthen (a person) mentally or morally, to increase the vigor of. |
| --- | --- |

# Flexible Approach

The paramount goal of the teaching work at the present time is to carry the Message of Bahá'u'lláh to every stratum of human society and every walk of life. An eager response to the teachings will often be found in the most unexpected quarters, and any such response should be quickly followed up, for success in a fertile area awakens a response in those who were at first uninterested.

The same presentation of the teachings will not appeal to everybody; the method of expression and the approach must be varied in accordance with the outlook and interests of the hearer. An approach which is **designed to appeal to everybody** will usually result in attracting the middle section, leaving both extremes untouched. No effort must be spared to ensure that the healing Word of God reaches the rich and the poor, the learned and the illiterate, the old and the young, the devout and the atheist, the dweller in the remote hills and islands, the inhabitant of the teeming cities, the suburban businessman, laborer in the slums, the nomadic tribesman, the farmer, the university student; all must be brought consciously within the teaching plans of the Bahá'í community.

Whereas plans must be carefully made, and every useful means adopted in the furtherance of this work, your Assemblies must never let such plans eclipse the shining truth expounded in the enclosed quotations: that it is the purity of heart, detachment, uprightness, devotion, and love of the teacher that attracts the divine confirmations and enables him,

however ignorant he be in this world's learning, to win the hearts of his fellowmen to the Cause of God.
    (**The Universal House of Justice**, *Wellspring of Guidance*, pp. 124-125)

We note that the new teaching methods you have developed, in reaching the waiting masses, have substantially influenced the winning of your goals, and we urge the American Bahá'ís, one and all, newly enrolled and believers of long standing, to arise, **put their reliance in Bahá'u'lláh** and armed with that supreme power, continue unabated their efforts to reach the waiting souls, while simultaneously consolidating the hard-won victories. New methods inevitably bring with them criticism and challenges no matter how successful they may ultimately prove to be. The influx of so many new believers is, in itself, a call to the veteran believers to join the ranks of those in this field  of service and to give wholeheartedly of their knowledge and experience. Far from standing aloof, the American believers are called upon now, as never before, to grasp this golden opportunity which has been presented to them, to **consult together prayerfully and widen the scope of their endeavours.**
    (**The Universal House of Justice**, *letter written to the National Spiritual Assembly of the United States, dated 14 February 1972*)

# Concerted and Persistent Efforts

Teaching the Faith embraces many diverse activities, all of which are vital to success, and each of which reinforces the other...

The aim, therefore, of **all Bahá'í institutions and**

**Bahá'í teachers is to advance continually to new areas and strata of society,** with such thoroughness that, as the spark of faith kindles the hearts of the hearers, the teaching of the believers continues until, and even after, they **shoulder their responsibilities as Bahá'ís and participate in both the teaching and administrative work of the Faith.**

There are now many areas in the world where thousands of people have accepted the Faith so quickly that it has been beyond the capacity of the existing Bahá'í communities to consolidate adequately these advances. The people in these areas must be progressively deepened in their understanding of the Faith, in accordance with well-laid plans, so that their communities may, as soon as possible, become sources of great strength to the work of the Faith and begin to manifest the pattern of Bahá'í life.

(**The Universal House of Justice**, *letter written to all National Spiritual Assemblies 25 May 1975*)

# Preventing Inoculation

The ... problem occurs most frequently in countries such as those in Africa, where there is entry by troops. In such countries it is comparatively easy to bring large numbers of new believers into the Faith, and this is such a thrilling experience that visiting teachers often tend to prefer to do this rather than help with the consolidation work... It should be pointed out that, especially if they [the traveling teachers] are assigned to expansion work, they must remember that consolidation is an essential and inseparable element of teaching, and if they go to a remote area and enrol believers whom no one is going to be able to visit again in the near future, they may well be doing a disservice to those people and to the Faith. To give people this glorious Message and then to leave them in the lurch, produces disappointment and disillusionment, so that, when it does become possible to carry out properly planned teaching in that area, the teachers may well find the people resistant to the Message. The first teacher who was careless of consolidation, instead of planting and nourishing the seeds of faith has, in fact, **"inoculated" the people against the Divine Message** and made subsequent teaching very much harder.

(**The Universal House of Justice,** *letter written on its behalf to all Continental Pioneer Committees dated 16 April 1981*)

 **Word Check**

| lurch | to abandon so that he is left in an awkward situation. |
|---|---|
| inoculate | to treat ( a person or animal) with vaccines or serums, etc., especially in order to protect against a disease. |

# Reinforcing the Administrative Foundations

This teaching work must include prompt, thorough and continuing consolidation so that all victories will be safeguarded, the number of Local Spiritual

Assemblies will be increased and the foundations of the Cause reinforced.

**(The Universal House of Justice**, *Naw-Rúz 1979 Message to the Bahá'ís of the World*)

Strengthening and development of Local Spiritual Assemblies is a vital objective of the Five Year Plan. Success in this one goal will greatly enrich the quality of Bahá'í life, will heighten the capacity of the Faith to deal with entry by troops which is even now taking place and, above all, will demonstrate the solidarity and ever-growing distinctiveness of the Bahá'í community, thereby attracting more and more thoughtful souls to the Faith and offering a refuge to the leaderless and hapless millions of the spiritually bankrupt, moribund present order.

**(The Universal House of Justice**, *Naw-Rúz 1974 Message to the Bahá'ís of the World*)

While this vital teaching work is progressing each National Assembly must ever bear in mind that **expansion** and **consolidation** are inseparable processes that must go hand in hand... To ensure that the spiritual life of the individual believer is continuously enriched, that local communities are becoming increasingly conscious of their collective duties, and that the institutions of an evolving administration are operating efficiently, is, therefore, as important as expanding into new fields and bringing in the multitudes under the shadow of the Cause.

**(The Universal House of Justice**, *a letter to all National Spiritual Assemblies engaged in mass teaching work dated 2 February 1966*)

Who can doubt that we are now entering a period of

unprecedented and unimaginable developments in the onward march of the Faith?... We know that the present victories will lead to active opposition, for which the Bahá'í world community must be prepared. We know the prime needs of the Cause at the moment: a vast expansion of its numbers and financial resources; a greater consolidation of its community life and the authority of its institutions; an observable increase in those characteristics of loving unity, stability of family life, freedom from prejudice and rectitude of conduct which must distinguish the Bahá'ís from the spiritually lost and wayward multitudes around them. Surely the time cannot be long delayed when we must deal universally with that entry by troops foretold by the Master as a prelude to mass conversion...

(**The Universal House of Justice**, *a letter to the Conference of the Continental Board of Counsellors dated 27 December 1985*)

# Processes of Entry by Troops

It has been due to the splendid victories in large-scale conversion that the Faith of Bahá'u'lláh has entered a new phase in its development and establishment throughout the world. It is imperative, therefore, that the process of teaching the masses be not only maintained but accelerated. The teaching committee structure that each National Assembly may adopt to ensure best results in the extension of its teaching work is a matter left entirely to its discretion, but an efficient teaching structure there must be, so that the tasks are carried out with dispatch and in accordance with the administrative principles of our Faith. From among the believers native to each country, competent traveling teachers must be selected and teaching projects worked out...

**(The Universal House of Justice**, *a letter to all National Spiritual Assemblies engaged in mass teaching work date 2 February 1966)*

The stage is set for universal, rapid and massive growth of the Cause of God. The immediate and basic challenge is pursuit of the goals of the Six Year Plan... The all-important teaching work must be imaginatively, persistently and sacrificially continued, ensuring the enrolment of ever larger numbers who will provide the energy, the resources and spiritual force to enable the beloved Cause to worthily play its part in the redemption of mankind.

**(The Universal House of Justice**, *Ridván 1987 Message to the Bahá'ís of the World)*

Over the last two years, almost one million souls entered the Cause. The increasing instances of entry by troops in different places contributed to that growth, drawing attention to Shoghi Effendi's vision which shapes our perception of glorious future possibilities in the teaching field. For he has asserted that the process of "entry by troops of peoples of divers nations and races into the Bahá'í world...will be the prelude to that long-awaited hour when a mass conversion on the part of these same nations and races, and as a direct result of a chain of events, momentous and possibly catastrophic in nature, and which cannot as yet be even dimly visualized, will suddenly revolutionize the fortunes of the Faith, derange the equilibrium of the world, and reinforce a thousandfold the numerical strength as well as the material power and spiritual authority of the Faith of Bahá'u'lláh." We have every encouragement to believe that large-scale enrolments

will expand, involving village after village, town
after town, from one country to another. However, it
is not for us to wait passively for the ultimate
fulfilment of Shoghi Effendi's vision. We few,
placing our whole trust in the providence of God and
regarding as a divine privilege the challenges which
face us, must proceed to victory with the plans in
hand.

    (**The Universal House of Justice**, *Ridván 1990 Message to the Bahá'ís of the World*)

# Summary

*What are the Processes?* A process is a series of actions or operations in achieving something. What does this mean in terms of growth of the Faith on a large scale? The answer is very clear. You may have noticed that in the previous extracts from the letters of the Guardian and the Universal House of Justice, certain ideas keep occurring time and again; each one explains the action or operation needed to expand the Faith on a large scale. Although each may be in the context of a particular phase, it can easily be applied to any of the three stages, namely, steady flow of reinforcements, entry by troops, and mass conversion. The following is a list of those processes:

- Only when the spirit has thoroughly permeated the world
- Promote love and unity
- Have a great ability for kindling in the hearts the love of God
- Spirit of real love for Bahá'u'lláh, for His Faith and its Institutions, and the believers for each other
- Mirror forth in their joint lives the exalted standards of the Faith
- Complete dedication, consecration to the noble mission
- The public sees in the Bahá'í Community a true pattern
- Animate their community life
- People of the world see a shining example
- Profound convulsions stir and rock the human race

- The maturity of the Bahá'ís within their communities, functioning according to Bahá'í laws and in the proper spirit of unity
- To advance continually to new areas and strata of society
- Shoulder their responsibilities as Bahá'ís and participate in both the teaching and administrative work of the Faith
- Men and women [the general population] are losing faith in human remedies
- Raise the intensity of teaching to a pitch never before attained
- Reach the minorities
- Universal participation
- Deepen their [newly enrolled believers'] knowledge and understanding of the Teachings
- Strengthen the functioning of their administrative institutions
- Greatly enrich the quality of Bahá'í life
- Embrace increasing numbers of people of capacity
- Designed [teaching methods] to appeal to everybody
- Put their [teachers'] reliance in Bahá'u'lláh
- Consult [Bahá'ís] together prayerfully and widen the scope of their endeavors
- Preventing inoculation
- Expansion
- Consolidation

# TEACHING BREAK

# 7

## More Teaching Tools

Like a craftsman (or craftswoman), we need a few more tools that we can reach for and use in our teaching activities. This chapter is a collection of various extracts from the Writings and a collection of useful information. It is not meant to be read from start to finish like previous chapters; rather, you may want to be of aware what is in it and use any portion of it as needed.  Here you will find:

- Inspirational words about the promises of ultimate victory
- Prayers to invoke divine help
- The history, laws, principles, and independent nature of the Faith
- Growth of the Faith
- World religions
- Social and economic activities
- Fundamental verities

## Promises of Ultimate Victory

God's plan never fails. In due course, Bahá'u'lláh's plans will have their full impact on all mankind, in the way past Revelations have changed life on this planet. Like many things of nature around us—such as the birds, flowers, trees, seasons, days, nights, stars, and galaxies—have a prescribed life cycle, which is marked by many developmental stages, so does the religion of God go through phases. In this

Dispensation we will witness wave after wave of victories in due course, according to the following promises:

## The Báb

Arise in His name, put your trust wholly in Him, and be assured of ultimate victory.
   (**Nabíl-I-A'Zam**, *The Dawnbreakers*, p. 94)

The Day is approaching when God will render the hosts of Truth victorious...
   (**The Báb**, *Selections from the Writings of The Báb*, p. 153)

O Lord! Assist those who have renounced all else but Thee, and grant them a mighty victory...
   (**The Báb**, *Selections from the Writings of The Báb*, p. 192)

## Bahá'u'lláh

Arise to further My Cause, and to exalt My Word amongst men. We are with you at all times, and shall strengthen you through the power of truth. We are truly almighty. Whoso hath recognized Me, will arise and serve Me with such determination that the powers of earth and heaven shall be unable to defeat his purpose.
   (**Bahá'u'lláh**, *Gleanings from the Writings of Bahá'u'lláh*, p. 137)

Should any one arise for the triumph of our Cause, him will God render victorious though tens of thousands of enemies be leagued against him. And if his love for Me wax stronger, God will establish his ascendancy over all the powers of earth and heaven. Thus have We breathed the spirit of power into all regions.

    (**Bahá'u'lláh**, *The World Order of Bahá'u'lláh*, p. 106)

## 'Abdu'l-Bahá

Should they show forth such a magnanimity, it is assured that they will obtain universal divine confirmations, the heavenly cohorts will reinforce them uninterruptedly, and a most great victory will be obtained.

    (**'Abdu'l-Bahá**, *Tablets of the Divine Plan*, revealed on April 5, 1916, p. 49)

And now you, if you act in accordance with the teachings of Bahá'u'lláh, may rest assured that you will be aided and confirmed. In all affairs which you undertake, you shall be rendered victorious, and all the inhabitants of the earth cannot withstand you. You are the conquerors, because the power of the Holy Spirit is your assistant.

    (*Star of the West*, Vol. 5 No. 8, p. 103)

## Shoghi Effendi

If one seeks the confirmations of the Holy Spirit, one can find it in rich abundance in the teaching field...and if the friends will arise with new determination, fully consecrated to the noble task ahead of them, victory after victory will be won for the Glorious Faith of God.

    (*The Individual and Teaching*, p. 29 or *The Power of Divine Assistance*, p. 56)

... the all-conquering potency of the grace of God,

vouchsafed through the Revelation of Bahá'u'lláh, will, undoubtedly, mysteriously and surprisingly, enable whosoever arises to champion His Cause to win complete and total victory.

(**Shoghi Effendi**, *Citadel of Faith*, p. 149)

### The Universal House of Justice

We are not alone nor helpless. Sustained by our love for each other and given power through the Administrative Order—so laboriously erected by our beloved Guardian—the Army of Light can achieve such victories as will astonish posterity.

(**The Universal House of Justice,** *Wellspring of Guidance*, p. 120)

...we must seize the opportunities of the hour and go forward confident that all things are within His mighty grasp and that, if we but play our part, total and unconditional victory will inevitably be ours.

(**The Universal House of Justice**, *Wellspring of Guidance*, p. 27)

 TEACHING MOMENT—TOO OLD OR

POOR TO BECOME A BAHÁ'Í?

I first heard the word "Bahá'í" near Sydney, Australia. My husband and I were visiting our daughter and son-in-law, who lived south of Sydney, and in a sightseeing trip, we saw this beautiful building. My son-in-law said that it was a Bahá'í Temple and would stop if I wished to take a picture (I still have it). There were some people busy around the building—mowing the grass, sweeping the walks, etc. I spoke to them and found out they included a bank manager, high school teacher, and a grandmother. I was impressed.

Then, for many years I didn't think of the Bahá'í Faith—or any other religion. My husband and I both quit our jobs to travel and build a retirement home. It was a wonderful time—no depression, no war, no children to raise, and if we were careful, enough money to get by. Also we were both in excellent health. Then the bottom dropped out of my world and I lost my beloved husband after two and a half years of illness. I was suddenly all alone. My daughter was physically far away and my son was emotionally far away.

Although I always knew there was a God, I did not believe in blind faith. Don't ask questions. I distrusted religious leaders who were always asking for money. I sure didn't have much after my husband's death.

I read a little about the Bahá'í Faith. One day I read in Era Banner, a Newmarket paper, that there was to be a Bahá'í public meeting in the library. So I went. I was invited to a fireside. I didn't know what it was all about. But the people seemed to be friendly. I asked about future meetings and they said they would send me a calendar, but they never did.

In 1992 I attended the hundredth anniversary of the Ascension of Bahá'u'lláh and was very impressed, not by the banquet, which was lovely, but by the people who attended, especially the ones at my table, who carried on a conversation with me.

I heard nothing more and I thought, "Well, maybe I am too old [72 years], too poor, or not their kind."

The next year, I read about a fireside in Aurora, the next town. I really wanted to become part of this faith that talks about the things that I hold dear—no prejudices, no hatred of people who are different, all one under God. So I attended the Aurora fireside—lovely people from many countries. But I never heard from them again.

I had been given a name and phone number at one time, so once again, I phoned. It was Vicky Hill. I was invited to a fireside and then a Feast. I was given material to read. After all my questions were answered, I became part of the Newmarket Bahá'í Community.

**Mary Austin,** Newmarket, Ontario, Canada

# Prayers for Teaching

Magnified be Thy name, O my God, for that Thou hast manifested the Day which is the King of Days, the Day which Thou didst announce unto Thy chosen Ones and Thy Prophets in Thy most excellent Tablets, the Day whereon Thou didst shed the splendor of the glory of all Thy names upon all created things. Great is his blessedness whosoever hath set himself towards Thee, and entered Thy presence, and caught the accents of Thy voice.

I beseech Thee, O my Lord, by the name of Him round Whom circleth in adoration the kingdom of Thy names, that Thou wilt graciously assist them that are dear to Thee to glorify Thy word among Thy servants, and to shed abroad Thy praise amidst Thy creatures, so that the ecstasies of Thy revelation may fill the souls of all the dwellers of Thine earth.

Since Thou hast guided them, O my Lord, unto the living waters of Thy grace, grant, by Thy bounty, that they may not be kept back from Thee; and since Thou hast summoned them to the habitation of Thy throne, drive them not out from Thy presence, through Thy loving-kindness. Send down upon them what shall wholly detach them from aught else except Thee, and make them able to soar in the atmosphere of Thy nearness, in such wise that neither the ascendancy of the oppressor nor the suggestions of them that have disbelieved in Thy most August and most mighty Self shall be capable of keeping them back from Thee.

(**Bahá'u'lláh**, *Bahá'í Prayers*, p. 169)

Praise be to Thee, O Lord my God! I implore Thee, by Thy Name which none hath befittingly recognized, and whose import no soul hath fathomed; I beseech Thee, by Him Who is the Fountainhead of Thy Revelation and the Dayspring of Thy signs, to make my heart to be a receptacle of Thy love and of remembrance of Thee. Knit it, then, to Thy most great Ocean, that from it may flow out the living waters of Thy wisdom and the crystal streams of Thy glorification and praise.

The limbs of my body testify to Thy unity, and the hair of my head declareth the power of Thy sovereignty and might. I have stood at the door of Thy grace with utter self-effacement and complete abnegation, and clung to the hem of Thy bounty, and fixed mine eyes upon the horizon of Thy gifts.

Do Thou destine for me, O my God, what becometh the greatness of Thy majesty, and assist me, by Thy strengthening grace, so to teach Thy Cause that the dead may speed out of their sepulchers, and rush forth towards Thee, trusting wholly in Thee, and fixing their gaze upon the orient of Thy Cause, and the dawning-place of Thy Revelation.

Thou, verily, art the Most Powerful, the Most High,
the All-Knowing, the All-Wise.
  (**Bahá'u'lláh**, *Bahá'í Prayers*, p. 170)

O my God, aid Thou Thy servant to raise up the Word,
and to refute what is vain and false, to establish
the truth, to spread the sacred verses abroad, reveal
the splendors, and make the morning's light to dawn
in the hearts of the righteous.

Thou art, verily, the Generous, the Forgiving.
  (**'Abdu'l-Bahá**, *Bahá'í Prayers*, p 174)

O God, my God! Aid Thou Thy trusted servants to have
loving and tender hearts. Help them to spread,
amongst all the nations of the earth, the light of
guidance that cometh from the Company on high.
Verily, Thou art the Strong, the Powerful, the
Mighty, the All-Subduing, the Ever-Giving. Verily,
Thou art the Generous, the Gentle, the Tender, the
Most Bountiful.
  (**'Abdu'l-Bahá**, *Bahá'í Prayers*, p 174)

O Thou incomparable God! O Thou Lord of the Kingdom!
These souls are Thy heavenly army. Assist them and,
with the cohorts of the Supreme Concourse, make them
victorious, so that each one of them may become like
unto a regiment and conquer these countries through
the love of God and the illumination of divine
teachings.

O God! Be Thou their supporter and their helper, and
in the wilderness, the mountain, the valley, the
forests, the prairies and the seas, be Thou their
confidant—so that they may cry out through the power
of the Kingdom and the breath of the Holy Spirit.

Verily, Thou art the Powerful, the Mighty and the Omnipotent, and Thou art the Wise, the Hearing and the Seeing.

('**Abdu'l-Bahá**, *Tablets of the Divine Plan*, revealed on April 8, 1916, p. 10)

 # Word Check

| | |
|---|---|
| **splendor** | brilliance, magnificent display or appearance, grandeur. |
| **summon** | to call upon a person to do something. |
| **import** | importance. |
| **fathom** | to get to the bottom of, to understand. |
| **sepulcher** | a tomb. |
| **splendor** | brilliance, magnificent display or appearance, grandeur. |
| **regiment** | a military unit of ground forces organized into two or more battalions. |
| **omnipotent** | having unlimited power. |

# History of the Faith

The following lists major events in a chronological order.

| Dates | Events |
|---|---|
| 1817 November 12 | Birth of Bahá'u'lláh in Núr, Persia |
| 1819 October 20 | Birth of the Báb in Shíráz, Persia |

| | |
|---|---|
| 1844 May 23 | Declaration of The Báb in Shíráz, Persia |
| 1844 May 23 | Birth of 'Abdu'l-Bahá in Tehran, Persia |
| 1850 July 9 | Martyrdom of the Báb in Tabríz, Persia |
| 1852 August | Bahá'u'lláh's imprisonment in Síyáh-Chál, Teheran |
| 1853 January 12 | Banishment of Bahá'u'lláh to Baghdád |
| 1853 April | Arrival of Bahá'u'lláh in Baghdád |
| 1854 April 10 | Withdrawal of Bahá'u'lláh to the mountains of Kurdistán |
| 1856 March | Return of Bahá'u'lláh to Baghdád |
| 1863 April 21 | Bahá'u'lláh's declaration of His Mission, to groups of Bábís, in the Ridván Garden in Baghdád |
| 1863 May 3 | Departure of Bahá'u'lláh from Baghdád |
| 1863 August 16 | Arrival of Bahá'u'lláh in Constantinople (now Istanbul) |
| 1863 December 12 | Arrival of Bahá'u'lláh in Adrianople (now Edirne) |
| 1868 August 31 | Bahá'u'lláh arrives in the prison city of 'Akká, Ottoman Palestine |
| 1870 June 23 | Death of Mírzá Mihdí, son of Bahá'u'lláh |
| 1873 | Marriage of 'Abdu'l-Bahá to Munírih Khánum |
| 1886 | Passing of Ásiyih Khánum, the wife of Bahá'u'lláh |
| 1888 March 29 | First public mention of Bahá'u'lláh and the Bahá'í Faith in the West, by E. G. Browne to the Essay Society, Newcastle-Upon-Tyne, England |
| 1891 | Bahá'u'lláh showed 'Abdu'l-Bahá the spot on Mount Carmel for the Shrine of the Báb |
| 1892 May 29 | Passing of Bahá'u'lláh at Bahji, near 'Akká |
| 1893 September 23 | First mention of the Faith in USA by Rev. George Ford. A paper was read on behalf of Rev. Henry Jessup mentioning the Faith. |
| 1897 March 1 | Birth of Shoghi Effendi |
| 1898 December 10 | The first western pilgrims arrived in 'Akká |
| 1901 August 20 | 'Abdu'l-Bahá was ordered confined to 'Akká by the Sultan of the Ottoman Empire |
| 1902 | Start of the construction of the first Bahá'í House of Worship in 'Ishqábád, Central Asia |
| 1908 July | The collapse of the Ottoman Empire resulted in the freedom of 'Abdu'l-Bahá |

| | |
|---|---|
| 1909 March 21 | The completion of the mausoleum of the Shrine of the Báb |
| 1910 August | 'Abdu'l-Bahá travels to Egypt |
| 1911 August | 'Abdu'l-Bahá's first visit to England |
| 1911 October | 'Abdu'l-Bahá's first visit to France |
| 1912 April 11 | 'Abdu'l-Bahá enters the port of New York |
| 1912 May 1 | 'Abdu'l-Bahá lays the foundation stone of the House of Worship in Wilmette |
| 1912 August 30 | 'Abdu'l-Bahá visits Canada |
| 1912 December 13 | 'Abdu'l-Bahá's second visit to England |
| 1913 January 21 | 'Abdu'l-Bahá's second visit to France |
| 1913 March 30 | 'Abdu'l-Bahá travels to Germany |
| 1913 April 9 | 'Abdu'l-Bahá goes to Austria and Hungary |
| 1913 December 5 | 'Abdu'l-Bahá returns to the Holy Land |
| 1916-1917 | 'Abdu'l-Bahá reveals the *Tablets of the Divine Plan* |
| 1920 April 27 | 'Abdu'l-Bahá is knighted by the British Government |
| 1921 November 28 | Passing of 'Abdu'l-Bahá in Haifa, Palestine, and His burial in the Shrine of the Báb. Shoghi Effendi becomes the Guardian of the Faith |
| 1925 May 10 | An Islamic Court in Egypt declares that the Bahá'í Faith is an independent religion |
| 1929 March 4 | A resolution of the Council of the League of Nations upholds the claim of the Bahá'í community to the House of Bahá'u'lláh in Baghdád |
| 1948 March | The Bahá'í International Community is registered as a non-governmental organization at the United Nations |
| 1949 April 30 | The Canadian Parliament incorporates the National Spiritual Assembly of Canada, the first such recognition of the Faith by a sovereign legislature |
| 1953 May 2 | Dedication of the first Bahá'í House of Worship in the West in Wilmette, Illinois, USA |
| 1957 November 4 | The passing of Shoghi Effendi in London |
| 1963 April 21 | The Universal House of Justice is elected for the first time. Six thousand Bahá'ís gather in London for the first Bahá'í World Congress |
| 1970 May | The Bahá'í International Community is granted |

|                    | consultative status with the Economic and Social Council (ECOSOC) of the United Nations |
|--------------------|---|
| 1979               | The Islamic revolution in Iran unleashed a new wave of persecution against the Bahá'í community in Iran |
| 1981               | The United Nations Sub-Commission on the Prevention of Discrimination and Protection of Minorities passed a resolution drawing attention to the persecution of Bahá'ís in Iran; 48 Bahá'í's are killed in Iran during the year |
| 1982 July 17       | The Seat of the Universal House of Justice is completed and inaugurated on Mt. Carmel, Haifa, Israel |
| 1985               | The United Nations General Assembly, for the first time, expresses concern over the situation of Iran's Bahá'ís in a resolution condemning Iran for human rights violations |
| 1985 October       | The Universal House of Justice issues *The Promise of World Peace*, a letter to the peoples of the world |
| 1992 May 29        | The second Holy Year begins as 3,000 Bahá'ís from 180 countries gather in Haifa to commemorate the 100th anniversary of the passing of Bahá'u'lláh |
| 1992 November 23-26 | An estimated 30,000 Bahá'ís gather in New York for the Second Bahá'í World Congress, the largest and most diverse gathering of Bahá'ís in history |

# Principles and Laws

## *Principles:*

- the oneness of God
- the oneness of religion
- the oneness of humanity
- the equality of women and men
- the elimination of prejudice

- the elimination of the extremes of wealth and poverty
- the independent investigation of truth
- universal education
- religious tolerance
- the harmony of science and religion
- a world commonwealth of nations
- a universal auxiliary language

## Do's:

- honesty
- trustworthiness
- chastity
- service to others
- purity of motive
- generosity
- deeds over words
- unity
- work as a form of worship

## Don'ts:

- killing
- stealing
- lying
- adultery and promiscuity
- gambling
- alcoholic drinks
- drug abuse
- gossip and backbiting

# Bahá'í Faith and Other Religions

Bahá'u'lláh teaches us that the Founders of all the major world religions, including

Abraham, Krishna, Moses, Zoroaster, Buddha, Jesus Christ, and Muhammad, are all Messengers from God. Their spiritual teachings are the same, but their social teachings differ according to the critical needs of each age They lived on earth. Referring to these religions, Bahá'u'lláh said:

> These principles and laws, these firmly established and mighty systems, have proceeded from one Source, and are the rays of one Light.
>
> (**Bahá'u'lláh**, *Gleanings from the Writings of Bahá'u'lláh*, pp. 287-288)

Among all the Prophets, Bahá'u'lláh has a special mission. He is the fulfillment of all the past Messengers and He started a new cycle in the history of mankind. The previous is the Adamic cycle, starting with Adam and finishing with Muhammad. This does not make Him any better than others; rather, He comes at a time when this transition is supposed to happen.

This section gives a brief description of some of the major religions of the world. Where possible, it also gives the relationship of Bahá'u'lláh to each past Prophet, copied from *The Bahá'ís*.

## *Krishna*

About 5,000 years ago, God sent His teachings through Krishna to the people of India. Krishna taught the people to know and love the one true God. He also taught them to respect and deal with the things of others as each would respect and deal with his own things.

Most of the people of India accepted Lord Krishna and His teachings. A magnificent civilization developed and flourished.

Krishna taught that God will send another Messenger. He said:

> Know thou that when virtues and justice decline in the world, and vice and injustice are enthroned, then I, the Lord, will make myself manifest as a

```
man amongst men, and ...I will destroy evil and
injustice...
```
   (*Bhagavad Gita*)

```
Conquer a man who never gives by gifts; subdue an
untruthful man by truthfulness: vanquish an angry
man by gentleness and overcome an evil man by
goodness.
```
   (*Mahabharata*)

To the Bahá'ís, Bahá'u'lláh comes as the new incarnation of Krishna, the "Tenth Avatar" and the "Most Great Spirit." He is "the birthless, the deathless," the One who, "when goodness grows weak," returns "in every age" to "establish righteousness" as prophesied in the Bhagavad Gita.

## Moses

Three thousand years ago, the Jewish people were in slavery in Egypt. God revealed Himself to Moses as a flame of fire in a bush. He told Moses to lead the people out of Egypt to Israel. God sent the ten commandments through Moses. We still follow these laws today.

The Jews followed Moses. They established a great civilization. God brought His truth to a troubled people. The power of this truth freed the Jewish people and brought them to the Promised Land.

God gave Moses a promise:

```
I will raise them up a prophet out of the midst of
their brethren like unto thee; and I will put my
words in his mouth, and he shall speak to them all
that I shall command him.
```

```
I am the Lord thy God, Which have brought thee out
of the land of Egypt, out of the house of bondage.
```

```
Thou shalt have no other gods before me.
```
  (*Exodus* 20:2,3)

To Bahá'ís, Bahá'u'lláh is the appearance of the promised "Lord of Hosts" come down "with ten thousands of saints." He is also a descendent of Abraham and a "scion from the root of Jesse." Bahá'u'lláh's exile from Iran to Israel is the fulfillment of numerous prophecies in the Bible and one of His missions is to lead the way for nations to "beat their swords into plowshares."

## Zoroaster

Zoroaster lived in Persia and wrote his thoughts in a book now called the *Ayvesta*, traced back to about the 6th century BC. He taught the existence of one true God, who is just and who will judge the living and the dead on the last day of time. He called for a ceremony of communion with God consisting of drinking some beverage, probably wine.

Zoroaster taught the people to follow the path of goodness, to speak the truth, to keep their promises and to do as they would like others to do unto you.

```
It is man's thought, words and deeds which carve
his destiny.
```
  (A*yvesta*)

Zoroaster also prophesied that in the future, God would send a Messiah who would unite all people and renew the world.

## Buddha

God chose Buddha to carry His Message to the people of Asia 2500 years ago. Buddha traveled throughout northern India. He had many followers. He taught the people to turn away from selfishness. It causes unhappiness. Happiness comes by desiring right living and right knowledge.

Hurt not others in ways that you yourself would
find hurtful.
   (*Tipitaka*)

Great civilizations were built on Buddha's teachings. Today more than 500 million people are Buddhists. The spirit of God shines through the teachings of Buddha.

Buddha foretold the coming of another Messenger like Himself. This Messenger, He said, would bring the age of unity.

To Bahá'ís, Bahá'u'lláh is the fulfillment of the coming of "a Buddha named Maitreye, the Buddha of universal fellowship." According to Buddhist tradition, He brings peace and enlightenment for all humanity.

## Jesus Christ

Two thousand years ago, a Messenger of God was born in the town of Bethlehem in what is now Israel. His name was Jesus. God sent His Revelation to Jesus: "And lo a voice came from heaven saying, 'This is my beloved Son in Whom I am well pleased'." After that time, He was known as Christ, which means the Anointed One.

Jesus the Christ traveled throughout Palestine teaching the people about God, the Almighty Father, the One Who had sent Him. He taught the people to love one another and to love God. He suffered and He died. He was crucified.

Great civilizations in the West were built upon His teachings. Today millions of people consider themselves Christians.

Jesus told the people that they could not understand everything He had to tell them. In the future, He said, "the Spirit of Truth" will come to guide them "unto all truth." Jesus was telling them that another Messenger would come. This Messenger would bring the Kingdom of God on Earth.

Our Father, Who art in Heaven. Hallowed be Thy
Name. Thy Kingdom come. Thy will be done on Earth
as it is in Heaven. Give us this day our daily
bread. And forgive us our trespasses as we forgive
those who trespass against us.

To Bahá'ís, Bahá'u'lláh is the fulfillment of Christ's promise to return "in the
Glory of the Father" and as a "thief in the night." The fact the Faith started in
1844 in itself relates to many Christian prophecies. In the 1840's, Africa
opened up to Christianity. Bahá'ís see this as the time when the Gospel had
been preached "to all nations" which coincides with the return of Christ.

## Muhammad

About 600 years after Christ died, God sent a Messenger to the warring tribes
of Arabia. These people were barbarians. They worshiped hundreds of idols
instead of the one God. God chose Muhammad to teach these people to know
Him and to love Him.

Muhammad's teachings helped warring tribes turn to God. They became a
nation. Moslem civilization made great discoveries and contributions to
science, mathematics, arts and literature. This is from the Qur'án:

How good is the reward of those who work, who
suffer patiently, who put their trust in their
Lord.

Muhammad promised that another Messenger would come after Him to renew
the religion of God. For Bahá'ís, Bahá'u'lláh fulfils the promise of the Qur'án
for the "Day of God" and the "Great Announcement," when God will come
down "overshadowed with clouds." Many events since 1844 can be related to
many traditional statements of Muhammad.

# TEACHING MOMENT—BURSTING
# WITH THE LOVE OF BAHÁ'U'LLÁH

After joining the Faith, I began teaching with a heart bursting with love of Bahá'u'lláh and the Faith. Incidently, I would have accepted Bahá'u'lláh even if He hadn't been the return of Christ; the fact He became only an added bonus for me.

Before all this happened, Dorothy Wingett used to talk about religion as we were both searching for something better. Although consciously I was not, for sure she knew she was looking for a new spiritual path. She was one of my first customers at my beauty shop, who also became my personal friend. Also, we had promised to each other that if one of us found something that made sense, we would share it with the other. So, of course, I could hardly wait to tell her the good news. Both Dorothy and her late mother Jean Northey were extremely versed in the Bible. I knew very little about it and was unable, with my limited knowledge, to convince them about Bahá'u'lláh's claims. In 1962, I sold my beauty shop and pioneered to Peterborough, just south of Lakefield, where they needed one more Bahá'í to form a Local Spiritual Assembly. It was formed in 1963, the year the first Universal House of Justice was elected, at the end of the Ten Year Crusade.

Dorothy and I drifted apart for a few years; however, during this time Gladys Tranter was also teaching Dorothy's mother, Jean Northey. Both lived in Woodview. Jean was so deepened in the Bible that she promised to live the rest of her life proving the Bahá'í Faith wrong. Both Dorothy and Jean attended firesides at Gladys' place, who showed self-sacrifice and patience as both were so adamant about disclaiming the truth of Bahá'u'lláh's mission. After some years, a book, *New Keys to the Book of Revelation,* by Ruth Moffett, was published. Gladys, Jean, and Dorothy studied it. After ten years, they finally realized that Bahá'u'lláh's claim was true. After accepting the Faith, both became dedicated servants of Bahá'u'lláh.

This bounty continued when Dorothy's father, Stan, her two sisters, Daphne Wilson, and June Scott, her daughter Cathy Wingett (married to a Bahá'í Steve Hayman), and her brother-in-law Ray Wingett, all accepted the Faith. Another blessing from God was that Dorothy and I are not only Bahá'í sisters and friends, but also are now sisters-in-law.

**Maddie Wingett**, Peterborough, Ontario, Canada

# Social and Economic Development

Historically, religion has played an important role in social and economic development of many countries around the world. In 1983 the Universal House of Justice initiated a global social and economic plan for the Bahá'í World Community. Because of a web of local and national administrative institutions around the world, the Faith is in a unique position to realize such a plan at a global scale. In the last fourteen years it has grown to about 1,344 projects of all types. Some of these programs are:

- Radio stations
- Health care
- Literacy programs
- Schools
- Tree planting
- Youth activities
- Women's activities
- Agricultural activities

Obviously, these projects are meant to infuse the Bahá'í principles and teachings into the world. This means promoting a holistic approach to solving human and social problems by applying spiritual principles to daily life. Some of the objectives are:

- Improve living conditions through education
- Teach self-reliance and self-sufficiency
- Resolve social problems through spiritual methods
- Encourage moral conduct that is consistent with the highest ideals of society
- Promote equality among all members of society, regardless of race, gender, religion, as a basis for justice

# Elements for a World Commonwealth

Over 100 years ago, Bahá'u'lláh envisioned a new world order, which will emerge with the following key building blocks:

- Recognized and secure borders for all nations
- Freedom of travel and thought for all peoples
- A general disarmament
- The establishment of a world federation of nations
- The establishment of a world tribunal for the adjudication of international disputes
- The creation of an international military force capable of enforcing the peace through the principles of collective security
- A commitment to the protection of cultural diversity

# What are the Fundamental Verities?

*From the Department of the Secretariat of the Universal House of Justice to an individual believer, 12 November 1996:*

With regard to your E-mail of 8 August 1996, we have been asked to say that it is true that Shoghi Effendi considered that his letter to the Bahá'ís of the West dated 8 February 1934 outlined certain fundamental verities of the Faith, and, therefore, it should be given primary importance in the

systematic study of the Cause. However, as you
further observe, the term is used in a variety of
contexts, since it also refers generally to the
basic beliefs, teachings, laws and principles of
the Faith. Three such instances help illustrate the
range of referents to which the Guardian was wont
to apply the term. First, he wrote in a letter to
the All-America International Teaching Conference
which gathered in 1953 that the House of Worship
is, "dedicated to the three fundamental verities
animating and underlying the Bahá'í Faith—the Unity
of God, the Unity of Prophets, the Unity of
mankind." Elsewhere, he emphasized that

> The education of the members of the community in
> the principles and essential verities underlying
> the Covenants of Bahá'u'lláh and of 'Abdu'l-Bahá
> as well as the Administrative Order of the
> Faith—the twin pillars sustaining the spiritual
> life and the institutions of every organized
> Bahá'í community—must, at all costs, be vigorously
> pursued and systematically intensified.

And in still another letter, the following
clarification is offered on behalf of Shoghi
Effendi:

> By "verity of the Faith" he means the great
> teachings and fundamentals enshrined in our Bahá'í
> literature; these we can find by reading the
> books, studying under Bahá'í scholars at summer
> schools and in classes, and through the aid of
> study outlines.

Moreover, the term fundamental verities was often
used in the correspondence of the Guardian when

introducing the basic aspects of the Faith in which all of the believers should be deepened and grounded, as for example:

Above all, the paramount duty of deepening the spiritual life of these newly fledged, these precious and highly esteemed co-workers, and of enlightening their minds regarding the essential verities enshrined in their Faith and its fundamental institutions, its history and genesis—the twin Covenants of Bahá'u'lláh and of 'Abdu'l-Bahá, the present Administrative Order, the Future World Order, the Laws of the Most Holy Book, the inseparable Institutions of the Guardianship and of the Universal House of Justice, the salient event of the Heroic and Formative Ages of the Faith, and its relationship with the Dispensations that have preceded it, its attitude towards the social and political organizations by which it is surrounded—must continue to constitute the most vital aspect of the great spiritual Crusade launched by the champions of the Faith from the shores of their native land....

Above all, the utmost endeavour should be exerted by your Assembly to familiarize the newly enrolled believers of the Faith, with the origins, the aims and purposes, as well as the processes of a divinely appointed Administrative Order, to acquaint them more fully with the history of the Faith, to instill in them a deeper understanding of the Covenants of both Bahá'u'lláh and of 'Abdu'l-Bahá, to enrich their spiritual life, to rouse them to a greater effort and a closer participation in both the teaching of the Faith and the administration of its activities, and to inspire them to make the necessary sacrifices for the furtherance of its vital interests. For as the body of the avowed supporters of the Faith is enlarged, and the basis of the structure of its Administrative Order is broadened, and the fame of the rising community spreads far and wide, a parallel progress must be achieved, if the fruits already garnered are to endure, in the spiritual quickening of its members and the deepening of their inner life.

As you can see, there is no absolute list of fundamental verities and the friends should not make an issue of this matter by attempting to codify these verities.

# Word Check

| systematic | methodical, according to a plan and not at random. |
|---|---|
| referent | what is symbolized by a word, etc. |
| sustain | to keep going continuously. |
| paramount | chief in importance, supreme. |
| fledged | mature, trained and experienced, *a full-fledged engineer.* |

# Summary

This chapter is a repository of useful information, containing two very vital resources: first, the promises of ultimate victories are sources of courage and, secondly, the prayers attract help and confirmation from the unseen spiritual world. The rest of its contents are used when presenting to those who are interested to know more about the Faith. By no means, do this and previous chapters discuss all the possible tools used for teaching the Faith; rather, it is only a beginning upon which one can build more resources.

# TEACHING BREAK

DON'T BE AFRAID TO TEACH! EVERYONE IS AN OPEN BOOK!

# Bibliography

**The Báb**

The Báb, *Selections from the Writings of the Báb*, Haifa: Bahá'i World Centre, 1976.

**Bahá'u'lláh**

Bahá'u'lláh, *Gleanings from the Writings of Bahá'u'lláh*, Wilmette, Illinois: Bahá'i Publishing Trust, 2nd Ed., 1976.
Bahá'u'lláh, *Hidden Words*, Taiwan: Bahá'i Publishing Trust, 1984.
Bahá'u'lláh, *Tablets of Bahá'u'lláh*, Haifa: Bahá'i World Centre, 1978.

**'Abdu'l-Bahá**

'Abdu'l-Bahá, *Foundations of World Unity*, Wilmette, Illinois: Bahá'i Publishing Trust, 1945.
'Abdu'l-Bahá, *Selections from the Writings of 'Abdu'l-Bahá*, Haifa: Bahá'i World Centre, 1978.
'Abdu'l-Bahá, *Tablets of the Divine Plan*, The National Spiritual Assembly of the Bahá'i of the United States, 1975.
'Abdu'l-Bahá, *Tablets of 'Abdu'l-Bahá*, Wilmette, Illinois: Bahá'i Publishing Trust, 2nd Ed., 1970.
'Abdu'l-Bahá, *The Secret of Divine Civilization*, Wilmette, Illinois: Bahá'i Publishing Trust, 1971.

**Shoghi Effendi**

Shoghi Effendi, *Citadel of Faith*, Wilmette, Illinois: Bahá'i Publishing Trust, 1970.
Shoghi Effendi, *God Passes By*, Wilmette, Illinois: Bahá'i Publishing Trust, 1974.
Shoghi Effendi, *Guidance for Today and Tomorrow*, Wilmette, Illinois: Bahá'i Publishing Trust, 1978.
Shoghi Effendi, *Advent of Divine Justice*, Wilmette, Illinois: Bahá'i Publishing Trust, 1971.
Shoghi Effendi, *The World Order of Bahá'u'lláh*, Wilmette, Illinois: Bahá'i Publishing Trust, 2nd Ed., 1974.

**The Universal House of Justice**

*Teaching the Bahá'i Faith*, Compiled by The Research Department of Universal House of Justice, 1995.
*The Individual and Teaching*, Compiled by The Research Department of Universal House of Justice, 1977.
*Wellspring of Guidance*, Wilmette, Illinois: Bahá'i Publishing Trust, 1969.


**Other**

*Bahá'i Prayers*, Wilmette, Illinois: Bahá'i Publishing Trust, 1991.
Balyuzi, H. M., *The Báb*, Oxford: George Ronald, 1974.
Balyuzi, H. M., *'Abdu'l-Bahá*, Oxford: George Ronald, 1973.
*The Bhagavad Gita*, Penguine Books, 1980.
Cobb, Stanwood, *Memories of Abdu'l-Bahá*, Los Angeles, CA: Kalimat Press, 1989.
Faizi, A. Q., *Stories from the Delight of Hearts*, New Delhi: Bahá'i Publishing Trust of India, 1969.
Honnold, Annamarie, *Vignettes from the Life of Abdu'l-Bahá*, Wilmette, Illinois: Bahá'i Publishing Trust, 1991.
Motlagh, Hushidar, *Teaching: The Crown of Immortal Glory*,
Nabíl-I-A`Zam, *Dawnbreakers*, Wilmette, Illinois: Bahá'i Publishing Trust, 1974.
*The Bahá'i*, Oakham, Leicestershire: Bahá'í Publishing Trust of the United Kingdom, 1994.
*The Bahá'í World*, Vol. IV, Oxford: George Ronald, 1981.
*Readings and Prayers*, Toronto, ON: The Board of Education for the City of Toronto, 1986.
*Star of the West*, Vol. III, Oxford: George Ronald, reprinted in 1978.
*Star of the West*, Vol. V, Oxford: George Ronald, reprinted in 1978
*Star of the West*, Vol. XIII, Oxford: George Ronald, reprinted in 1978

# Index

**213**